Advanced Introduction to the Sociology of the Self

Elgar Advanced Introductions are stimulating and thoughtful introductions to major fields in the social sciences, business and law, expertly written by the world's leading scholars. Designed to be accessible yet rigorous, they offer concise and lucid surveys of the substantive and policy issues associated with discrete subject areas.

The aims of the series are two-fold: to pinpoint essential principles of a particular field, and to offer insights that stimulate critical thinking. By distilling the vast and often technical corpus of information on the subject into a concise and meaningful form, the books serve as accessible introductions for undergraduate and graduate students coming to the subject for the first time. Importantly, they also develop well-informed, nuanced critiques of the field that will challenge and extend the understanding of advanced students, scholars and policy-makers.

For a full list of titles in the series please see the back of the book. Recent titles in the series include:

Cybersecurity Law
David P. Fidler

The Sociology of Work
Amy S. Wharton

Marketing Strategy
George S. Day

Scenario Planning
Paul Schoemaker

Financial Inclusion
Robert Lensink, Calumn Hamilton and Charles Adjasi

Children's Rights
Wouter Vandenhole and Gamze Erdem Türkelli

Sustainable Careers
Jeffrey H. Greenhaus and Gerard A. Callanan

Business and Human Rights
Peter T. Muchlinski

Spatial Statistics
Daniel A. Griffith and Bin Li

The Sociology of the Self
Shanyang Zhao

Advanced Introduction to

The Sociology of the Self

SHANYANG ZHAO

Professor of Sociology, Department of Sociology, Temple University, USA

Elgar Advanced Introductions

Edward Elgar
PUBLISHING

Cheltenham, UK • Northampton, MA, USA

Published by
Edward Elgar Publishing Limited
The Lypiatts
15 Lansdown Road
Cheltenham
Glos GL50 2JA
UK

Edward Elgar Publishing, Inc.
William Pratt House
9 Dewey Court
Northampton
Massachusetts 01060
USA

A catalogue record for this book
is available from the British Library

Library of Congress Control Number: 2022937626

ISBN 978 1 80037 533 8 (cased)
ISBN 978 1 80037 535 2 (paperback)
ISBN 978 1 80037 534 5 (eBook)

Printed and bound in Great Britain by TJ Books Limited, Padstow, Cornwall

Contents

Figures

About the author

Shanyang Zhao is Professor of Sociology at Temple University, with a secondary appointment at the Center for Asian Health in the Lewis Katz School of Medicine at Temple University. He received his Ph.D. in sociology from the University of Maryland at College Park. Prior to joining the Temple faculty in 1997, he worked as a senior research associate in the Institute for Social Research at the University of Michigan. His research interests include social psychology, new media, and metatheory. His recent publications have appeared in *Philosophical Psychology, New Ideas in Psychology, Symbolic Interaction*, and *European Journal of Social Theory*.

Acknowledgments

This book is dedicated to the memory of the late Professor Morris Rosenberg, whose graduate seminar on the sociology of self-concept piqued my initial interest in the study of the self. I took his seminar when I was a doctoral student in the Department of Sociology at the University of Maryland, College Park. One day in class, I asked Professor Rosenberg a question about the difference between self and self-concept. He looked at me, smiling, and said: "I know what self-concept is, but I am not sure what self is. Maybe someday you will be able to find it out." After class, Professor Rosenberg invited me to his office and lent me several books on the conceptualization of self/self-concept/identity. After completing my coursework, I took a preliminary exam on self-concept, and Professor Rosenberg served as chair on my examination committee. In the years since then, Professor Rosenberg's seminar and the many talks I had with him have continued to inspire me in my own research on the sociology of the self, which culminates in the publication of this book.

I also am indebted to Professor George Ritzer, my doctoral advisor, for his mentorship and his guidance on my study of sociological metatheory. I did not have time to work on the publication of my dissertation because I moved into a new area of inquiry for postdoctoral work right after graduating from the Ph.D. program. However, my doctoral training in metatheorizing has benefited my subsequent research in multiple fields, including the sociology of the self.

My thanks are also due to Stephen Harries, Editor at Edward Elgar Publishing, for reaching out to me with a suggestion that I do a book on the sociology of the self for the Elgar Advanced Introductions series. Without the much-needed push from him, it would probably be years before I would find the time to write this book. I would also like to acknowledge the support provided by a sabbatical leave awarded to me by Temple University.

I also wish to thank Routledge for its permission to adapt my article "What is reflective self-awareness for?" published in *Philosophical Psychology* 31(2), 2017:187-209, for use in this book (chapter 6).

Last but not least, I thank my wife, Yuheng Wu, and my son, Sihai Dave Zhao, for their love and support.

1 Introduction to *The Sociology of the Self*

What is the self? How is the self formed? And why does the self matter? This book provides concise but not simple answers to these three questions from the sociological standpoint. Although a lot of research has been done on the sociology of the self, no consensus has been reached among sociologists on their answers to these questions. In addressing these questions, this book introduces readers to the central issues sociologists have been grappling with and the accomplishments they have achieved in understanding the phenomenon of the self. It is hoped that this introductory text will serve as a useful roadmap to the sociology of the self and generate further interest in research on the relationship between self and society.

1.1 Overview of classic works

While human curiosity about the phenomenon of the self can be traced all the way to antiquity,[1] it is generally held that the scientific inquiry of self began with the publication of William James's seminal book, *The Principles of Psychology*, in 1890.[2] In the chapter on "The Consciousness of Self," James defined what the self is, described how it is constituted, and explained why it is important. James differentiated between one's self-consciousness, which he called the "I," and the self that one is conscious of, which he called the "me." The self is what "I" calls "me" or what one recognizes to be oneself. In other words, the self is an empirical entity one perceives and acts toward, rather than a stream of consciousness that flows inside one's head. According to James, the empirical self is composed of three parts: the "material me" that includes one's body and material possessions, the "social me" that includes one's reputation and social standing, and the "spiritual me" that includes one's dispositions, beliefs, and values. James argues that the self is important because it affects one's feelings and guides one's behavior. For the first time in human self-inquiry, the phenomenon of the self was defined in a way that it became amenable to empirical examination. Since then, research on the self has emerged in many fields across disciplines.

In 1902, the sociologist Charles Cooley published a monograph, *Human Nature and the Social Order*,[3] in which he devoted two chapters to the re-examination of William James's conception of the social self, which was a part of the empirical self. Applying the first-person perspective of the "I," James defined the self as an entity that one recognizes to be oneself or "me," but in the process of delineating the constituents of the empirical self, James would sometimes deviate from the first-person perspective and switch to the third-person point of view, whereby producing conceptual inconsistencies. For example, James described the social self of the individual as "his image in the eyes of his own 'set'" so that the individual "has as many different social selves as there are distinct groups of persons about whose opinions he cares."[4] However, James did not explain how one comes to know one's image in the eyes of others, for what others think of oneself (the third-person point of view) is not necessarily the same as what one thinks others think of oneself (the first-person point of view).[5]

In his book, Cooley corrected this conceptual inconsistency by introducing the famous metaphor of the "looking-glass self." Cooley points out that one's social self comes from one's *imagination* of one's appearance to another person and one's *imputation* of the other person's judgment of that appearance, and he calls the resulting self-image one attains the "reflected or looking-glass self."[6] Thus, this social self is not what others think of oneself, but what one thinks others think of oneself. Even though it may not correspond to one's actual image in the eyes of others, this imagined or imputed self-image nonetheless influences one's self-feelings, such as pride or shame, and, subsequently, affects how one acts toward oneself and others.

Building on Cooley's clarification of the social self, George Mead (1934) made a number of new advancements in the sociology of the self in his published lecture notes, *Mind, Self, and Society*.[7] Mead examined the phenomenon of the self from the standpoint of social behaviorism which treats humans as a species of organisms that shares the attributes of many other social organisms. A key difference between humans and nonhuman social animals, according to Mead, is that humans possess selves while other social animals do not. "Having a self," as Mead puts it, means that the organism is able to "become an object to itself," that is, the organism is "both subject and object."[8] Mead believes that humans are the only species that have selves because only humans have the mental capacity to reflect on their own existence.

However, Mead argues that the possession of the reflexive mental capacity in itself does not produce the self, for the genesis of the self also requires the social condition of interacting with other members of society. As the metaphor of the looking-glass self illustrates, an individual comes to possess the self by taking the attitudes of others toward the individual. In his book, Mead further improved on Cooley's theory of reflected appraisal by identifying the stages through which the self develops in the early years of the individual's life. Mead distinguishes between two types of "others" who come to affect the formation of one's self: (a) the significant others and (b) the generalized other. The *significant others* are particular individuals whose opinions one cares about and trusts, and the *generalized other* is the attitude of the community of which one is a member. The formation of the self goes through two main stages: the *"play stage"* in which the self is primarily affected by the attitudes of one's significant others, followed by the *"game stage"* in which the attitude of the generalized other begins to exert more influence.

One of the many other important contributions Mead made was that he looked into not only the social impact on the self but also the social functions of the self. Mead was concerned with the issue of the source of "novelty" in self-perception. He reasons that if the self were entirely a reflection of others' attitudes toward the individual, then the individual would have no agency and revelation in self-understanding, and ultimately it would be difficult to explain the origins of, and changes in, one's attitudes toward others and oneself. To address this issue, Mead separated the "I" from the "me" and considered the "I" to be a source of novelty that enables the individual to respond creatively, and sometimes rebelliously, to the influence of others. Just as the individual's self-perception is affected by the attitudes of others, "the attitude of the other is changed through the attitude of the individual" (Mead 1934: 179),[9] which, in turn, may change the attitude of the community of which the individual is a part. As such, the self of the individual is not merely a social product passively reflecting the attitudes of others, but also a social force that actively impacts on oneself, others, and the larger social environment.

Inspired by Mead's insight on the agency of the individual in shaping the attitudes of others, Erving Goffman (1959) developed a theory of the dramaturgical self in his influential book, *The Presentation of Self in Everyday Life*.[10] Nearly reversing the proposition of Cooley's looking-glass self, Goffman argues that the attitudes of others toward the individual are in fact shaped by the individual's presentation of self. According to Goffman, the self is not a hidden entity to be discovered but a personal character to be performed: "it is a dramatic effect arising diffusely from a scene that is presented,"[11] and the presentation of the individual "leads the audience to impute a self to a performed character."[12] That is to say, what others think of the individual is largely determined by how the individual performs in the presence of others, and the self is the impression of the individual the performance generates on others. As to what is behind the mask one is wearing or what the individual really is, Goffman's answer is that neither the individual nor the audience knows for sure. Of course, Goffman did not deny the impact of others on self-perception, especially, during the formative years of the individual, his intention was to draw attention to the effect of the individual's self-conscious action on the social perceptions of others. The inclusion of self-conscious action in the phenomenon of the self considerably broadens the scope of the study of the self and enriches the understanding of the relationship between self and others.

More recently, the British sociologist Anthony Giddens (1991) devoted a monograph to the study of the self in modern times: *Modernity and Self-Identity*,[13] in which he examined the impact of late modernity on the transformation of what he called "self-identity." Self-identity, according to Giddens, "is not a distinctive trait, or even a collection of traits, possessed by the individual. It is the self as reflectively understood by the person in terms of her or his biography."[14] Self-identity is therefore the identification of one's own existence informed by one's biographical experience. While the use of the first-person point of view to define the self has followed the Jamesian tradition, there is a subtle but important difference between self and self-identity that Giddens fails to distinguish: self is the *entity* one perceives to be oneself, whereas self-identity is "a *concept* of a person"[15] or *self-concept*. Self and self-concept are not the same thing. Nevertheless, Giddens's point was that the arrival of the era of "high modernity" transformed the self-identity of the individual through the influence of mass media and other emergent electronic technologies, and this transformation was being reflected in individuals' presentations of their selves in the different regions of their lives, including their bodily appearance and demeanor.

Besides the works reviewed above, a huge amount of research on the self has been carried out in sociology on both empirical and theoretical grounds, and considerable progress has been made in the conceptualization of self and the understanding of the social factors that shape the formation of the self.[16] However, a number of important issues remain unresolved. Perhaps top on that list is the distinction between self and self-concept. In sociological research, self has often been equated to self-concept and also used interchangeably with identity or self-identity.[17] What is really at issue here is not just a definitional matter, for the differences in definition have direct implications for theory and research: if self is defined as something that is more than self-concept, it would then be necessary to specify what the other parts of the self are so that they can be studied as well.

Another major issue is the identification of the mechanisms of self-concept formation and the conditions under which each mechanism operates. "Reflected appraisal" is the most well-known mechanism derived from Cooley's looking-glass self metaphor, and it has been used to explain almost all aspects of self-concept formation. The mechanism of "social comparison" has sometimes been used as a counterargument to the principle of reflected appraisal.[18] Besides the need to specify the scope conditions of the mechanisms that are already known, efforts should be made to identify new mechanisms that account for the effects of other social factors such as mass media, the influence of which can be found in nearly all aspects of social life.

The third issue has to do with the social functions of the self. This issue is closely related to the agency-structure or micro–macro linkage problem that sociologists have been grappling with for a long time.[19] The self is not merely a social product, passively reflecting the attitudes of others, but is also a social force that plays an active role in social life. The examination of the social functions of the self needs to go beyond the study of its impact on the behavior or self-presentation of the individual to examine the role the self plays in the constitution of human society. As Mead puts it, the self of the individual affects not just the individual but also the society of which the individual is a part.

Finally, the understanding of the human self is limited without comparative analysis of cross-species differences. Since the 1970s, a growing amount of evidence has been found indicating that humans are not the only species in the animal kingdom that possess selves, and a lot of research have been done to find out where humans and nonhuman animals differ in the capacities for self-reflection and self-regulation.[20] The sociology of the self must take into account this growing body of literature in examining the uniqueness of human selves and their impacts on society.

1.2   Special features of this book

Building on the foundation of the classic works, this book introduces a broader conceptualization of self that extends beyond the scope of self-concept, and it regards the self as both a product of social influence and a force that affects the constitution of human society. In particular, this book is marked by the following key features:

1. Adhering to the *first-person point of view* adopted in the classic works, this book defines the self as an entity that the individual reflects upon and acts toward as their own existence. This conception of self as one's perceived own existence includes self-concept but extends beyond it.

2. The self is regarded as part of a larger constellation of related phenomena named in this book the "*self-phenomenon.*" The self-phenomenon includes four principal components: the empirical existence of the individual in society, self-concept, self-conscious action, and the self proper; in addition, there are three psychosocial processes that connect these four components: self-reflection, self-regulation, and self-verification which includes conceptual adjustment and self-enactment. The combination of those components and processes constitutes a self-directed feedback system that guides the individual's dealings with self and others in society. To have a self is to have all those constituent parts, and to understand the self is to understand the self-phenomenon as a whole.

3. Factors that influence the formation of the self are divided into two large categories: neurocognitive prerequisites and social determinants. *Neurocognitive prerequisites* of the self are the neurological and psychological conditions that provide the individual with the capacities for self-reflection and self-regulation. Those capacities themselves are not the self, but rather the conditions that are necessary for the self to emerge. *Social determinants* of the self, on the other hand, are sociocultural factors, such as interpersonal, institutional, cultural characteristics of the society, that shape the formation of the self. The sociological study of the self involves the examination of the social determinants of the self.

4. Specifically, this book looks at the influences of two social structural factors on the constitution of the self: *social schemas* and *social resources*. In the study of the impact of social schemas on self-concept, a distinction is made between determinants and mechanisms, with the latter referring to the concrete *processes* by which the former exerts its impact. *Cultural conditioning* is introduced, in addition to reflected appraisal and social comparison, as the third mechanism by which social schemas affect the formation of self-concept. In the study of the impact of social resources on self-conscious action, the effects of social position and social capital on the perceived and actual self-efficacy are examined.

5. This book also examines the social functions of the self. The focus of examination is on the roles the self plays in *human cooperative activity* through which human society is created, maintained, and transformed. Two types of human selves are distinguished: situational and normative, which are needed for two distinct modes of human collaboration. The *situational self* is necessary for human cooperative activity in transient and evolving situations, whereas the *normative self* is required for institutional construction, a societal feature that is uniquely human. Thus, it is argued that just as there is no self without society, there is no human society without human selves.

6. Finally, the distinctiveness of the roles the human selves play in human cooperative activity is examined in the context of *cross-species comparisons*. Humans are not the only species that possess selves, and not all animal societies need selves either. It is the possession of the language-based normative self by the human individual that makes institutional regulation possible and human society unique.

1.3   Organization of the book

Chapter 2 introduces the *sociological perspective* on the self. The self-phenomenon has been studied by different disciplines and each discipline provides a unique perspective on the self. To help understand the characteristics of the sociological disciplinary perspective, the basic structure of a scientific discipline is examined, and the uniqueness of the sociological perspective is described in comparison to those of the related disciplines. The perspective of phenomenology is discussed in greater detail because it is particularly relevant to the study of the self-phenomenon.

Chapter 3 addresses the question of *what the self is*. It introduces the concept of the *emic self*, which is *the entity that one takes to be oneself*. The emic self is part of the self-phenomenon that includes three other components: the empirical existence of the individual, self-concept, and self-conscious action, each of which consist of subcomponents. These constituent parts are linked together by a set of reflective and regulative psychosocial processes, including conceptual adjustment and self-enactment, to form a self-directed feedback system that guides the activities of the individual toward self and others.

Chapter 4 addresses the question of *how the self is formed*. It focuses on the impact of two social structural factors – social schemas and social resources – on the constitution of the self. It takes a closer look at three mechanisms by which social schemas shape the formation of self-concept: reflected appraisal, social comparison, and cultural conditioning, paying special attention to the scope conditions under which each mechanism of self-concept formation operates. It also examines the ways in which social resources affect the individual's self-conscious action through the mediation of social position and social capital.

Chapter 5 addresses the question of *why the self matters* or *what the self is for*. There is little doubt that the self affects the behavior of the individual, but not enough attention has been paid to the impact of the self on society. This chapter argues that the self affects not just the behavior of the individual but also the human cooperative activities through which human society is created, maintained, and transformed. Human cooperative activity requires that human individuals are mutually responsive to one another's intention and action at the self-consciousness level, and capable of regulating their collaborative activities based on institutional rules that they construct themselves. The possession of the language-based normative self by the individual makes institutional regulation of social live possible.

Chapter 6 examines cross-species differences in the constitution of society. It differentiates animal societies into three types – caste, individualized, and alliance societies – and shows that while all societies need a social recognition module for conspecific collaboration, only individuals in alliance animal society have the capacity for self-recognition. Self-recognition enables individuals to form transient coalitions with selective conspecific members to deal with evolving and unpredictable social situations. Human society is a form of alliance society as well, but humans possess normative selves which allow them to engage in institutionalized cooperative activity whereas individuals in other alliance societies possess only situational selves for transient and situation-based collaborations.

The epilogue concludes the book by highlighting the key arguments made in the preceding chapters with some reflections on the implications of those arguments for personal well-being and sociological theorizing.

Notes

1. Jerrold Seigel (2005) *The Idea of the Self: Thought and Experience in Western Europe since the Seventeenth Century*. Cambridge: Cambridge University Press.
2. William James (1950 [1890]) *The Principles of Psychology* (Vol. 2). New York: Dover.
3. Charles H. Cooley (1956 [1902]) 'Human nature and the social order,' in R. C. Angell (ed.), *The Two Major Works of Charles H. Cooley: Social Organization [and] Human Nature and the Social Order*. Glencoe, IL: Free Press, pp. 1–451.
4. William James (1950 [1890]), pp. 294–295.
5. For more discussions on this inconsistency, see Shanyang Zhao (2014) 'Self as an emic object: A re-reading of William James on self,' *Theory & Psychology*, 24(2), 199–216.
6. Charles H. Cooley (1956 [1902]), p. 184.
7. George H. Mead (1934) *Mind, Self, and Society: From the Standpoint of a Social Behaviorist*. Chicago: The University of Chicago Press.
8. Ibid., p. 137.

9.   Ibid., p. 179.
10. Erving Goffman (1959) *The Presentation of Self in Everyday Life*. New York: Doubleday.
11. Ibid., p. 253.
12. Ibid., p. 252.
13. Anthony Giddens (1991) *Modernity and Self-Identity: Self and Society in the Late Modern Age*. Stanford, CA: Stanford University Press.
14. Ibid., p. 53.
15. Ibid.
16. For reviews of research in sociology on the self, see Morris Rosenberg (1981) 'The self-concept: Social product and social force,' in M. Rosenberg and R. Turner (eds.), *Social Psychology: Sociological Perspectives*. New York: Basic Books, pp. 593–624; Karen A. Cerulo (1997) 'Identity construction: New issues, new directions,' *Annual Review of Sociology*, 23, 385–409; Peter L. Callero (2003) 'The sociology of the self,' *Annual Review of Sociology*, 29, 115–133.
17. For introductory texts on the sociology of the self, see Viktor Gecas and Peter J. Burke's (1995) 'Self and identity,' in K. S. Cook, G. A. Fine, and J. House (eds.), *Sociological Perspectives on Social Psychology*. Boston: Allyn and Bacon, pp. 41–67; Jan E. Stets and Peter J. Burke (2003) 'A sociological approach to self and identity,' in M. R. Leary and J. P. Tangney (eds.), *Handbook of Self and Identity*. New York: The Guilford Press, pp. 128–152; John P. Hewitt (2007) 'Self and its social setting,' in J. P. Hewitt, *Self and Society: A Symbolic Interactionist Social Psychology*. Boston, MA: Allyn and Bacon, pp. 79–140; Kent L. Sandstrom, Kathryn J. Lively, Daniel D. Martin, and Gary Alan Fine (2014) 'The nature and significance of the self,' in K. L. Sandstrom, K. J. Lively, D. D. Martin, and G. A. Fine, *Symbols, Selves, and Social Reality: A Symbolic Interactionist Approach to Social Psychology and Sociology*. Oxford: Oxford University Press, pp. 123–163.
18. See Viktor Gecas and Michael L. Schwalbe (1983) 'Beyond the looking-glass self: Social structure and efficacy-based self-esteem,' *Social Psychology Quarterly*, 46, 77–88.
19. Jeffrey C. Alexander, Bernhard Giesen, Richard Munch, and Neil J. Smelser (eds.) (1987) *The Micro–Macro Link*. Berkeley: University of California Press.
20. For an early groundbreaking article, see Gordon G. Gallup (1970) 'Chimpanzees: Self-recognition,' *Science*, 167, 86–87; and for more recent developments, see Herbert S. Terrace and Janet Metcalfe (eds.) (2005) *The Missing Link in Cognition: Origins of Self-Reflective Consciousness*. Oxford: Oxford University Press.

2 Sociological and related perspectives[1]

The self-phenomenon is a subject matter of sociological inquiry, but sociology is not the only discipline that studies the self-phenomenon. Why is a phenomenon amenable to the examination of multiple disciplines? How does the sociological perspective differ from those of the other disciplines in the study of the self-phenomenon? To answer these questions, one needs to know the general structure of a scientific discipline, the principal factors that determine the uniqueness of a disciplinary perspective, and the interconnections among disciplines that make their perspectives complementary to one another.[2] This chapter addresses these issues in an effort to articulate the main characteristics of the sociological perspective.

2.1 The structure of a discipline

A scientific discipline is an intellectual endeavor that aims to identify and understand a distinctive class of phenomena. A class of phenomena consists of a multitude of properties, and the property that distinguishes one class of phenomena from others constitutes the distinctive attribute of the given class of phenomena. No matter how different they may be, phenomena of the same class all possess the same distinctive attribute. For example, the key attribute that distinguishes vertebrates from invertebrates is that all vertebrate animals have a backbone inside their body, and vertebrates can be further divided into five subgroups based on additional attributes: fish, amphibians, reptiles, birds, and mammals. A preliminary task of disciplinary research is to identify and delineate the distinctive attribute of the class of phenomena that the discipline is supposed to investigate.

Once a unique class of phenomena is identified and delineated for a discipline, the discipline can then be divided into three analytically distinct realms or domains based on whether that class of phenomena is treated as a dependent variable or an independent variable in the studies (see Figure 2.1).[3] A dependent variable, also called "explanandum" or "explicandum," is a phenomenon to be explained or accounted for, and an independent variable, also called "explanans" or "explicans," is a phenomenon that is used to explain other phenomena. In *realm I*, which is the primary domain of a discipline, one part of the discipline-specific phenomena is used to explain the other parts of the same class of phenomena. Such studies are useful for understanding relationships among the different parts of a distinctive class of phenomena, but they are "tautological" in the sense that they are unable to account for the origin and change of the concerning *class* of phenomena. *Realm II* picks up what realm I leaves off by using the classes of phenomena studied by other disciplines as the independent variable to account for the class of phenomena specific to the concerning discipline. In *realm III*, however, the class of phenomena studied by the concerning discipline is used as the independent variable to explain the classes of phenomena unique to other disciplines.

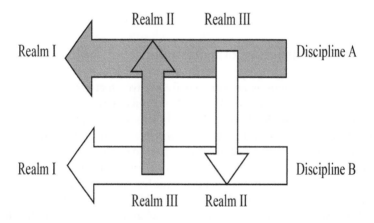

Figure 2.1   The structure of a discipline

The German sociologist Max Weber (1949), for example, used a similar classification scheme to describe the disciplinary structure of economics.[4]

Weber starts by defining the distinctive attribute of economy as "the scarcity of means." Events that are created or used for the purpose of dealing with economy are called *economic phenomena*. Examples of economic phenomena are the stock exchange and the banking world. The study of the economic phenomena per se constitutes the realm of the economics proper. The discipline of economics, according to Weber, also includes the study of two other types of phenomena: (1) *economically relevant* phenomena such as religion and politics which are not economic phenomena in themselves but have economic significance, i.e., have influence on economic processes; and (2) *economically conditioned* phenomena such as the artistic interest of the public and the political state of a nation, which are things affected by the economic processes. According to this tripartite taxonomy, the study of the economic phenomena per se constitutes realm I of economics, and the study of the economically relevant phenomena and the economically conditioned phenomena constitute realm II and realm III of economics, respectively.

Of the three disciplinary realms, realm I is the discipline proper and constitutes the distinctive *perspective* of the discipline. Delineation and understanding of the relationships among the various parts of the discipline-specific class of phenomena become the focus of research in this realm. Realms II and III are multidisciplinary in nature, for they involve the application of the perspectives of multiple disciplines to the study of different classes of phenomena. In realm II, the perspectives of other disciplines are employed to investigate the class of phenomena specific to the concerning discipline; in realm III, on the other hand, the perspective of the concerning discipline is employed to investigate the classes of phenomena specific to other disciplines. As it were, different disciplines become increasingly interconnected through the development of their respective realms II and III, forming an ever-expanding network of multidisciplinary research fields (see Zhao 1993).[5]

2.2   The sociological perspective

Sociology studies a class of phenomena that can be broadly defined as "inter-organism behavior regularity" (Wallace 1991: 31),[6] where "organisms" include humans and nonhuman social animals (thereafter referred to as "social animals"). "Inter-organism behavior regularity" refers to patterns of interaction and relationship among members of society. In the case of human society, "joint or collective action constitutes the domain of sociological concern, as exemplified in the behavior of groups, institutions, organizations, and social classes" (Blumer 1969: 16).[7] The central issues that concern sociologists include: What is society for? What makes society possible? Why is a society organized in the way it is? And how does society change?

In realm I, sociologists seek to delineate and understand different forms of the "social," ranging in scope and complexity from sociality to societality. At the level of *sociality*, sociologists are interested in interactions among individuals and the resulting patterns of interpersonal relationship. The focus of their study is the ways in which individuals come to fit their lines of action to one another based on their interpretations of the situation in which the interaction takes place. At the level of *societality*, on the other hand, sociologists seek to find out how humans construct institutional rules to regulate their societal activities. "Societal" is different from "social" in that the former refers to a collectivity of competing individuals living together in a territory for survival and thrival, whereas the latter mostly involves interpersonal interaction and relationships within a collectivity. In human society, societal activities are regulated by institutional rules consisting of "the beliefs and modes of behavior instituted by the collectivity" (Durkheim 1982: 45).[8] Given that the institutional regulation of social life is unique to human society, sociology has also been "defined as the science of institutions, their genesis and their functioning."[9] The actual research practice in realm I of sociology, however, involves the study of human interaction and relationship at all levels, including the middle-range activities and events that connect micro sociality and macro societality.[10] The predominant theories from this realm constitute the dominant sociological perspective of the discipline.

In realm II, sociologists attempt to explain patterns of human interaction and relationship in terms of the attributes of other classes of phenomena to which sociological phenomena are believed to be etiologically related. Humans are biological organisms and therefore are subject to biological laws. Humans are also conscious beings whose behaviors are mediated by the internal psychological processes. Equally important, humans live in the ecological and technological environments which serve as the material conditions for human survival and thrival. Therefore, to fully understand the ways in which humans interact with one another and regulate themselves, all these factors have to be taken into account. Geological, biological, and psychological studies of the patterns of human interaction and relationship are examples of such multidisciplinary endeavors.

Finally, in realm III, patterns of human interaction and relationship are used to account for variation and change in other classes of phenomena. This category of phenomena consists of anything that is subject to the influence of the patterns of human interaction and relationship. Broadly speaking, it includes (1) human activities in specific domains of social life, e.g., politics, economy, family, education, religion, and law; (2) human relationships of various types, such as race, ethnicity, gender, class, urbanicity, and nation-states; and (3) emergent social and environmental problems or issues such as substance abuse, the COVID-19 pandemic, pollution, and global warming. Sociological studies of the impact of the established patterns of human interaction and relationship on those phenomena constitute the different branches of applied sociology, such as political sociology, sociology of family, sociology of education, sociology of religion, urban sociology, and environmental sociology.

It should be noted that there are two different types of "sociological study of xxx," with "xxx" denoting any class of phenomena amenable to socio-logical explanation. The first type of study aims to demonstrate the causal influence of a given sociological variable on *any* non-sociological varia-bles, whereas the objective of the second type of study is to investigate the causal relevance of *any* sociological variables to a given non-sociological variable. The subtle difference between the two lies in the fact that in the first type of study a given sociological independent variable is chosen first and a non-sociological dependent variable is selected afterwards to show the causal efficacy of the chosen sociological independent variable; in the second type of study, on the other hand, a given non-sociological depend-ent variable is chosen first and a set of sociological independent variables are then screened in search of a possible causal influence. In other words, the first type of study is explanans-oriented whereas the second type of study is explanandum-oriented.

Aneshensel et al. (1991),[11] for example, have differentiated between *soci-ological* and *sociomedical* models in the study of the social characteristics of mental health. They point out that sociomedical models are *disorder specific* in the sense that the mental health impact of a set of sociological variables is assessed only with regard to a particular mental disorder;

sociological models, in contrast, are *risk-factor specific* in the sense that the mental health impact of a set of sociological variables is assessed with regard to *any* mental disorder. Because of the restrictions imposed on the selection of the dependent variable, Aneshensel et al. argue that sociomedical models are "inherently inadequate" for identifying the mental health consequences of sociological variables. The distinction between these two types of studies is important for demarcating the disciplinary nature of multidisciplinary subfields. Technically speaking, the second type of study belongs to realm II of the neighboring disciplines. In the case of the mental health research, sociomedical models are best seen as part of realm II of the medical sciences.

Sociology of the self is a branch of applied sociology. Like any other phenomenon, the self-phenomenon can be studied by multiple disciplines. The sociological study of the self seeks to explain the self-phenomenon in terms of the characteristics of the interaction and relationship the individual engages in with other members of society. The characteristics of social interaction and relationship include patterns of sociality at the micro level and institutional arrangements at the macro level. In the disciplinary context of sociological study, the self can be examined either as a dependent variable affected by the characteristics of society, or as an independent variable affecting the characteristics of society. Most of the existing sociological research on the self has treated the self-phenomenon as a dependent variable, and the self as an independent variable has not been well studied in sociology.

This book focuses on the study of the self from the sociological perspective, and it examines the self-phenomenon as a dependent variable as well as an independent variable. Specifically, the study consists of three parts. In part I, it defines and delineates the self, differentiating it from and relating it to other constituent parts of the self-phenomenon, such as self-reflectivity, self-concept, and self-conscious action. In part II, it examines how the characteristics of social structure in the form of social schemas and social resources affect the formation and transformation of the self. And in part III, it looks at the importance of the self for the constitution and functioning of human society, paying special attention to the roles the self plays in both situational and normative human cooperative activities.

2.3   Other related perspectives

While primarily applying the perspective of sociology to the study of the self, this book also utilizes the perspectives of some related disciplines. In particular, the perspectives of psychology, social psychology, evolutionary biology, and phenomenology will be touched upon to varying degrees in the examination of the self.

2.3.1   Psychology

Psychology is a scientific discipline that studies the phenomenon of mind and behavior.[12] Realm I of the discipline focuses on the mental processes of the individual which include, among other things, consciousness, thoughts, feelings, attitudes, and motivations. Realm II of the discipline examines the factors that affect the mental processes of the individual, such as the neurological foundation of the mind and the social environment that influences the content of the mind. And realm III of the discipline studies how the mind, along with other factors, affects the individual's behavior, personality, and relationships with others.

The psychological perspective is important for the study of the self. Reflective self-awareness – a psychological prerequisite of having a self – is a mental attribute that is unique to the human species and a few select social animals. The cognitive, affective, and evaluative aspects of the self, e.g., self-cognition, self-emotion, and self-valuation, are mental processes that fall in the domain of psychological investigation.[13]

2.3.2   Social psychology

Social psychology is the joint application of the perspectives of sociology and psychology to the study of the phenomena of interpersonal relationships. As a field of interdisciplinary research, social psychology has been described as having multiple subareas or "faces."[14] Using the tripartite classification scheme introduced at the beginning of this chapter, three subdomains of social psychology can be identified: social psychology proper, psychological social psychology, and sociological social psychology.[15] *Social psychology proper* studies the sociality of human interaction and relationship, with symbolic interactionism being a major theoretical perspective.[16] This branch of social psychology might be regarded as belonging to realm I of sociology, focusing on human interaction and relationship at the micro level, which includes face-to-face interaction, interpersonal relationship, and small group dynamics. *Psychological social psychology* examines the impact of psychological variables, e.g., individual perception, thought, feeling, and personality on the sociality of human interaction and relationship.[17] *Sociological social psychology*, on the other hand, focuses on the influence of the macro-level societal variables, e.g., social stratification, organizational culture, and the structure of institutions, on the micro-level human interaction and relationship.[18]

A considerable part of the sociological study of the self falls in the realm of social psychology. In a way, it can be argued that the self is a social psychological phenomenon which is shaped by the psychological factors on the one hand and the sociological factors on the other. The perspective of psychological social psychology is important for the examination of the influence of perception, attitudes, and personality on the formation of the self, and the perspective of sociological social psychology contributes to the understanding of the impact of social stratification, organization, and institutions on the structure of the self.

2.3.3   Evolutionary biology

Evolutionary biology studies the origin and diversification of organisms over time. The diversity of life on earth is accounted for in terms of the adaptation of organisms, through genetic and cultural changes, to the varying local environments for survival and reproductive success.[19] This evolutionary process is also responsible for the emergence of the different species of social animals that compete and cooperate with one another in society.

Self-awareness is a distinctive mental attribute possessed only by certain select species of social animals, such as dolphins and chimpanzees besides humans.[20] What is the adaptive function of self-awareness for social life? How do human selves differ from animal selves? What roles does self-awareness play in the functioning of animal and human societies? Such questions cannot be adequately addressed without utilizing the perspective of evolutionary biology.

2.3.4   Phenomenology

Phenomenology is a branch of philosophy that studies the objectivity of human experience and knowledge. It starts with the argument that humans come to know things as they appear in human experience, in other words, as "phenomena" or appearances of things, not as "nomena" or things as they really are. Appearances of things are objects of sense and are comprehended based on the experience of the perceiver. This argument raises a fundamental question about the objectivity of human knowledge: How can humans know what an object really is if they come to know it only as it appears in their experience which mediates their perception and understanding? Depending on how this question is answered, there are different schools of phenomenological thought.[21]

The application of phenomenological reasoning to the study of the human social world gives rise to phenomenological sociology. The human social world consists of people interacting with one another. If each person comes to know the world as it appears in the person's unique experience, how is it then possible for one person to see the world as it is seen by another person? Moreover, if different persons experience the world in different ways, how is mutual understanding – which is essential to social life – possible? The phenomenological sociologist Alfred Schutz (1967)[22] answers this question by dividing the human social world into four spatial-temporal zones: predecessors, consociates, contemporaries, and successors, and argues that people achieve mutual understanding in different ways in those different zones.

The application of phenomenological reasoning to the self-knowledge of the individual gives rise to the phenomenology of self. A critically important concept of phenomenological analysis is the *first-personal point of view*, or the "egocentric" standpoint of the perceiver. As the phenomenologist Zahavi (2003)[23] explains, the world is experienced by an individual from the perspective of the individual, and it is impossible for anyone to see the world in any other way. Zahavi calls this egocentric nature of individual perception the "first-personal givenness of experience."[24] According to Zahavi (2009), this first-personal givenness enables the individual to differentiate between the self and the rest of the world, for the individual will have a sense of "me-ness" or "mineness" when the self is being perceived.[25] This ability is innate to perception as consciousness, according to Zahavi, is at the same time self-consciousness. However,

Zahavi is quick to add that this is only a "minimal level" of self-consciousness, presumably universal to all conscious organisms.

This phenomenological perspective is very important for the sociological study of the self. In particular, it is impossible to correctly define the self in the absence of the first-person point of view. The self is the entity the individual recognizes to be "me" or "mine" while experiencing the world from the egocentric standpoint. This definition of the self raises a question about the differences among individuals in their egocentric standpoints. Given that the first-person point of view gives rise to the self, what factors shape the first-person point of view? Different individuals perceive the world, including themselves, differently, but such differences cannot be fully accounted for by biology and psychology. Sociology has a lot to contribute to the understanding of the *social causes* of the differences in the first-person points of view of the individuals.

Another issue related to the phenomenological argument is the concept of "me-ness" or "mineness." Assuming it is true that all conscious organisms have a "minimal level" of self-awareness, how is the self-awareness of social animals different from that of nonsocial animals? And how is human self-awareness different from animal self-awareness? It has been argued in the literature that while all animals have bodily self-awareness, only humans and a few select species of social animals have reflective self-awareness, i.e., the awareness of others' attitudes toward oneself. However, it remains unclear how human selves differ from the selves of the select species of social animals. Drawing on the insights from phenomenological reasoning, this book addresses those questions from the sociological perspective.

2.4   Conclusion

The above discussion indicates that a full understanding of the complex self-phenomenon would require the collaboration of a lot of disciplines. There is an ancient Indian parable about a group of blind people trying to figure out what an elephant is really like by individually groping its parts. In a way, the self-phenomenon is akin to the elephant in the parable and the multitude of relevant disciplinary perspectives are the separate gropes of the blind people. While limited in its scope, each disciplinary perspective sheds unique light on the self-phenomenon. This book aims to provide a sociological take on the phenomenon of the self. The next chapter embarks on this challenging intellectual journey by seeking to first define and delineate the attributes and structure of the self.

Notes

1. Part of the material discussed in this chapter comes from an article previously published by the author: Shanyang Zhao (1993) 'Realms, subfields, and perspectives: On the differentiation and fragmentation of sociology,' *The American Sociologist*, 24(3/4), 5–14.
2. "Perspective" is used here to refer to "approach," "orientation" or other similar concepts.
3. For more discussions on disciplinary structures and interdisciplinary relationships, see Shanyang Zhao (1993).
4. Max Weber (1949) *The Methodology of Social Sciences*. Ed. and tr. E. A. Shils and H. A. Finch. Glencoe, IL: The Free Press.
5. Shanyang Zhao (1993).
6. Walter Wallace (1991) 'Toward a disciplinary matrix in sociology,' in N. J. Smelser (ed.), *Handbook of Sociology*. Newbury Park, CA: Sage, pp. 23–76.
7. Herbert Blumer (1969) *Symbolic Interactionism: Perspective and Method*. Berkeley: University of California Press.
8. Emile Durkheim (1982) *The Rules of Sociological Method and Selected Texts on Sociology and its Method*. Ed. S. Lukes, tr. W. D. Halls. New York: The Free Press.
9. Ibid., p. 45.
10. Jeffrey C. Alexander, Bernhard Giesen, Richard Munch, and Neil J. Smelser (eds.) (1987) *The Micro–Macro Link*. Berkeley: University of California Press.
11. Carol S. Aneshensel, Carolyn M. Rutter, and Peter A. Lachenbruch (1991) 'Social structure, stress, and mental health: Competing conceptual and analytic models,' *American Sociological Review*, 56, 166–178.
12. David G. Myers (2011) *Psychology*. New York: Worth.
13. Mark R. Leary and June Price Tangney (eds.) (2012) *Handbook of Self and Identity*. New York: The Guilford Press.
14. Sheldon Stryker (1977) 'Developments in "two social psychologies": Toward an appreciation of mutual relevance,' *Sociometry*, 40, 145–160; James S. House (1977) 'The three faces of social psychology,' *Sociometry*, 40, 161–177; Robert G. Boutilier, J. Christian Roed, and Ann C. Svendsen (1980) 'Crises in the two social psychologies: A critical comparison,' *Social Psychology Quarterly*, 43, 5–17.
15. It should be noted that the division of social psychology into these three subdomains is a result of following the established convention of treating social psychology as a separate disciplinary field. In fact, the intersection of

sociology and psychology produces two, rather than three, interdisciplinary research fields: socio-psychology which studies psychological phenomena from the standpoint of sociology, and psycho-sociology which studies sociological phenomena from the standpoint of psychology. However, this symmetrical rule does not always work. For example, sociology of medicine makes sense, but medicine of sociology does not. This is because while sociological phenomena are believed to influence medical practice, medical practice is normally not seen as accountable for patterns of human interaction and relationship.

16. Herbert Blumer (1969).
17. John D. Delamater and Daniel J. Myers (2011) *Social Psychology*. Belmont, CA: Thomson Wadsworth.
18. Morris Rosenberg and Ralph H. Turner (eds.) (1981) *Social Psychology: Sociological Perspectives*. New York: Basic.
19. John T. Bonner (1988) *The Evolution of Complexity*. Princeton, NJ: Princeton University Press.
20. Herbert S. Terrace and Janet Metcalfe (eds.) (2005) *The Missing Link in Cognition: Origins of Self-Reflective Consciousness*. Oxford: Oxford University Press.
21. Dermot Moran (2000) *Introduction to Phenomenology*. New York: Routledge.
22. Alfred Schutz (1967) *The Phenomenology of the Social World*. Tr. G. Walsh, F. Lehnert, and G. Walsh. Evanston, IL: Northwestern University Press.
23. Dan Zahavi (2003) 'Phenomenology of self,' in T. Kircher and A. David (eds.), *The Self in Neuroscience and Psychiatry*. Cambridge: Cambridge University Press, pp. 56–75.
24. Ibid., p. 59.
25. Dan Zahavi (2009) "Is the self a social construct?" *Inquiry*, 52(6), 551–573.

Further reading

Blumer, Herbert (1969) *Symbolic Interactionism: Perspective and Method*. Berkeley: University of California Press.
Delamater, John D. and Daniel J. Myers (2011) *Social Psychology*. Belmont, CA: Thomson Wadsworth.
Moran, Dermot (2000) *Introduction to Phenomenology*. New York: Routledge.
Ritzer, George and Jeffrey Stepnisky (2017) *Sociological Theory*. Thousand Oaks, CA: Sage.
Zhao, Shanyang (1993) 'Realms, subfields, and perspectives: On the differentiation and fragmentation of sociology,' *The American Sociologist*, 24(3/4), 5–14.

3 Emic conception of the self

In the social sciences it is not uncommon for scholars to disagree among themselves on the key concepts that define the very subject matter of their disciplinary research. This is also true for the study of the self, except that in this case the disagreement over the definition of the self is much more striking because the self is such a ubiquitous phenomenon in everyday life that everyone seems to know what it is. Although they intuitively know what the self is, people have great difficulty in defining this phenomenon precisely. Scholars have been struggling with this concept as well. It is not just that different researchers tend to define the same concept in different ways, but that "sometimes individual writers have used *self* in more than one way within a single article or chapter" (Leary and Tangney 2012: 4).[1]

A major factor responsible for this conceptual conundrum is the attempt to define the self in the same way that most other phenomena are defined in science and everyday life. That common method is the use of the objective "third-person perspective," which defines an object in terms of its distinctive attributes assessed from the standpoint of an objective observer, or the "third person." For example, cats are defined by their feline traits and dogs by their canine characteristics, and these attributes can be empirically observed and differentiated by an unbiased researcher. However, this is not how the self should be defined, for the self is essentially a "first-person object," which means that it can be observed as such only by the person whose self it is. Just as the reflection of an object cannot be explained without reference to the source object whose reflection it is, the self is definable only from the perspective of the individual whose self it is. Put in generic terms, *the self is what an entity takes to be itself.* Such is the case of the "me," which is what the "I" recognizes to be itself. There are only a few select species of organisms on this planet, humans included, that are known to have an "I" that is capable of recognizing itself. To define the self is, therefore, to take the perspective of the "I."

This chapter begins with a brief overview of the common conceptions of self, followed by the introduction of a set of conceptual tools that are subsequently used to depict and define the phenomenon of self. Specifically, this chapter presents an *emic conception* of the self that defines the self from the "first-person point of view."[2] Self-conscious individuals in society come to possess selves by reflecting upon and acting toward what they consider to be their own existence. *The self is the object that one takes to be oneself.* It is the mistake of attempting to define the self in the absence of this first-person perspective that has resulted in various conceptual confusions about the self and the difficulties in understanding it.

3.1   Common conceptions of the self

The *self* is often mistaken by laypeople for the "soul" of a person or the "homunculus," i.e., a little figure, inside the head that influences the person's thought and action. Within the scientific community, definitions of the self vary both within and across disciplines. Olson (1998)[3] has documented eight different connotations of the self in philosophy, and Neisser (1988)[4] has identified five distinct types of "self-knowledge" being studied by psychologists. In sociology, there have also existed a number of conceptions of self that are associated with different schools of social thought.[5] The following four concepts of self are among the most common in the social sciences: self as self-reflectivity, self as self-concept, self as public persona, and self as the individual.

3.1.1   Self as self-reflectivity

This usage is most prevalent in psychology. Many psychologists regard the self as "the set of psychological mechanisms or processes that allows organisms to think consciously about themselves" (Leary and Tangney 2012: 6).[6] *Self-reflectivity* refers to the mental capacity of making oneself the object of one's attention and reflection, a cognitive ability that is believed to be possessed only by humans and a few other select species in the animal kingdom. Similar concepts include self-awareness, self-consciousness, and self-perception. Another mental capacity often associated with self-reflectivity is the "executive function" that enables self-conscious organisms to regulate their behavior according to the standards they set for themselves, as opposed to being dictated by instincts, impulses, or external stimuli (Baumeister and Vohs 2012).[7] This ability is also termed *self-regulation* or *self-control* (Carver and Scheier 1998).[8] Modern advances in neuroscience have enabled researchers to look for the neural structure that underlies the processes of self-reflection and self-regulation.[9]

3.1.2   Self as self-concept

This usage is common in sociology. Instead of seeing the self as a capacity for, or the process of, self-reflectivity, many sociologists regard the self as "a product of this reflexive activity," i.e., "the concept the individual has of himself as a physical, social, and spiritual or moral being" (Gecas 1982: 3).[10] According to this definition, self is the same as self-concept, which refers to "the totality of the individual's thoughts and feelings with reference to oneself as an object" (Rosenberg 1986: 7).[11] Self-identity, self-image, and self-schema are terminologies that have been seen as interchangeable with self-concept. This notion of self focuses on the mental images and related feelings that individuals have in regard to themselves, rather than the mental capacities and the underlying neurological foundations that make self-representation and self-feeling possible. The bulk of the sociological study of the self has been devoted to the examination of the social and cultural factors that shape the formation and transformation of an individual's self-concepts.[12]

3.1.3   Self as public persona

This usage frequently appears in the fields of social psychology and sociology. It places emphasis on the presentational nature of the self. As a public persona, the self of the individual emerges from interactions with others. The possession of the capacity for self-reflectivity and the resulting self-concept are mainly for the purposes of helping individuals interact with others in society. Through social interaction, an individual develops a self or public persona that distinguishes the individual from other members of society. However, this self is not "something housed within the body of its possessor," but rather "a dramatic effect arising diffusely from a scene that is presented, and the characteristic issue, the crucial concern, is whether it will be credited or discredited" (Goffman 1959: 253).[13] According to this definition, the self is neither a reflective capacity nor a self-concept, but "a performed character" to be imputed to the individual by others based on the individual's dramaturgical performance (p. 252). Self-presentation, self-actualization, and self-enactment are concepts that are closely associated with this conception of self.

3.1.4 Self as the individual

This connotation is implicit in many of the usages of self across different disciplinary fields. Acknowledging that the self is a "surprisingly quirky" and "notoriously evasive" concept, the psychologist Jerome Bruner (2003: 209) once remarked jokingly that "the best we seem able to do when asked what it is is to point a finger at our forehead or our chest."[14] Humor aside, Bruner implies that the self is no other than the individual. Jerrold Seigel (2005: 3), a historian, makes explicit this implied notion of self by providing a formal definition that directly equates the self with the individual or the person:

> By "self" we commonly mean the particular being any person is, whatever it is about each of us that distinguishes you or me from others, draws the parts of our existence together, persists through changes, or opens the way to becoming who we might or should be.[15]

This definition includes in the notion of self all aspects of the existence of an individual, i.e., not just the individual's body but also their thoughts, activities, possessions, and relationships over the entire lifespan – the individual's past, present, and future. The totality of an individual's existence makes the individual a unique person, distinguishable from all other individuals.

While each of the above four conceptions contains some element of truth about the self, none is satisfactory. Indeed, *self-reflectivity* is a mental capacity essential for the individual to have a self in the same sense that eyes are indispensable for a person to see, but just as eyes are not equal to what a person sees, self-reflectivity is not synonymous with the object that the individual reflects upon and acts toward as their own existence. *Self-concept* and self are also closely related, but again they are not the same thing. The difference between the two is akin to the difference between the image of an apple one has in the head and the actual apple one perceives; in other words, the mental representation of an object is not the same as the perception of the actual object. One's *public persona* can be a part of one's self if one identifies oneself with what one presents to others, but in reality one's public self-presentation does not always reflect what one thinks one is. Moreover, one's "real" self includes what one hides behind one's public façade and the other aspects of one's life that one is conscious of but unable to manipulate. Related to this notion of self is the concept of self-presentation, a form of *self-conscious action* which is essential for the construction and maintenance of self.

Finally, the individual per se is not the individual's self, for the existence of the individual must be perceived and acted upon by the individual as the individual's own existence in order for it to become the self of the individual. As observed by George Mead (1934: 142), a founder of the sociology of the self, "the individual is not a self in the reflective sense unless he is an object to himself."[16] The self is not an entity in itself, but an entity that becomes an object to itself through self-reflection and self-regulation. For this reason, any attempt to "lodge the self in a structure" that lacks self-reflectivity is doomed to fail:

> For any posited structure to be a self, it would have to act upon and respond to itself – otherwise, it is merely an organization awaiting activation and release without exercising any effect on itself or on its operation. (Blumer 1969: 63)[17]

In other words, objects per se are not selves. To have a self, an object must possess the capacity for self-awareness and self-regulation – the ability to reflect upon and act toward its existence, for the self is no other than the object that becomes an object to itself. The self thus defined is called here the *emic object* or the *emic self*.[18]

3.2   Self as an emic object

To better explicate the notion of self as an emic object, it is necessary to introduce a set of conceptual tools that can be used to construct a first-personal framework for understanding the constitution of self. Such instrumental concepts include (a) first- and second-order objects, (b) etic and emic standpoints, and (c) first-person perspective.

3.2.1   First- and second-order objects

First-order objects are things as they are, and second-order objects are things as they are perceived.[19] *Things as they are* can be either material (e.g., rocks and animals) or ideational (e.g., beliefs and values) objects. *Things as perceived* result from the combination of things as they are and the perception of them by a perceiver who employs a certain perceptual apparatus or "lens." A perceptual apparatus is comprised of several parts: the *perceptual instrument*, naked or technologically mediated; the *perceptual standpoint* or the location – physical or social – from which the perception is attained; and the *perceptual schema*, e.g., the stock of knowledge and experience that helps the perceiver interpret the obtained sensory data. Because of the inevitable influence of the perceptual apparatus on the perception of objects, second-order objects always differ from their first-order counterparts. The aim of science is to make the second-order objects as close to the first-order objects as methodologically possible.

3.2.2   Etic and emic standpoints

Based on the standpoint of the perceiver from which the perceptions are attained, second-order objects are further divided into two subtypes: *etically perceived* and *emically perceived*. Initially coined by the linguist Kenneth Pike (1967)[20] and further refined by the anthropologist Marvin Harris (1976),[21] *etic* means "from outside" and *emic* "from within." Correspondingly, the *etic standpoint* refers to the point of view *from outside*, which stands in contrast to the *emic standpoint* – the point of view *from within*. In the anthropological study of a village, for example, researchers from outside of the village perceive the village etically, whereas residents of the village perceive their own village emically. Both standpoints have their perceptual advantages as well as blindsight. Generalizing this distinction to the perception of any object, the etic perception of an object is the perception of the object by other objects from outside, and the emic perception of an object is the perception of the object by the object itself from within, i.e., the object's *self-perception*.

3.2.3   First-person perspective

Needless to say, not all objects have the capacity to perceive, and not all perceiving objects have the capacity to self-perceive. *Self-perception* means that the perceiver not only makes itself the object of its own perception but also recognizes that what it perceives is itself. While all sentient beings are capable of perceiving, only a few select social species in the animal kingdom, humans included, have the ability to self-perceive, with the level of this ability varying across species ranging from bodily self-awareness to reflective self-consciousness (Barresi and Moore 1996).[22] In the case that an organism is able to become an object to itself, the organism is said to possess a *first-person perspective*, which enables a social organism to perceive and recognize itself as a unique individual.[23] There are two distinctive levels of the first-person perspective: (a) prelinguistic and intuitive versus (b) linguistic and narrative, with the latter allowing individuals to communicate their self-conceptions to others explicitly.[24] Some social animals have been found to have the prelinguistic first-person perspective, but it is generally believed that only humans possess the narrative first-person point of view.

In humans, the first-person perspective emerges in the early years of an individual's life (Harter 1999).[25] Through linguistic communication with other members of society, children develop the ability to conceptualize and make references to themselves from the first-person point of view – initially the perspective of the first-person singular "I" and later the perspective of the first-person plural "we." The "me" or "mine" that the individual refers to as one's own existence from the first-person perspective constitutes the individual's *emic self*.[26]

3.3   The self-phenomenon

The emic self is not a stand-alone object, but rather an integral part of a larger constellation of related phenomena that enable individuals to perceive and regulate their existence in society. This constellation of phenomena centers around the *empirical existence* of the individual in society. As a member of the human species, the individual is endowed with the capacities for *self-reflection* and *self-regulation*, both are to be activated and developed in society. The capacity for self-reflection enables the individual to form a *self-concept* or self-image by examining and reflecting on one's own empirical existence, and the capacity for self-regulation, on the other hand, allows the individual to maintain or change one's perceived own existence through *self-conscious action*, or self-action for short. The *self* is the resulting object that the individual reflects upon and acts toward as one's own existence in society. The individual is constantly engaged in a process of *self-verification* to make sure that there is a correspondence between self and self-concept, and that any perceived discrepancy be removed through either *perceptual adjustment* or *self-enactment*. This constellation of interrelated phenomena centering on the empirical existence of the individual is named here the *self-phenomenon.* The relationships among the constituent parts of the self-phenomenon are depicted in Figure 3.1.

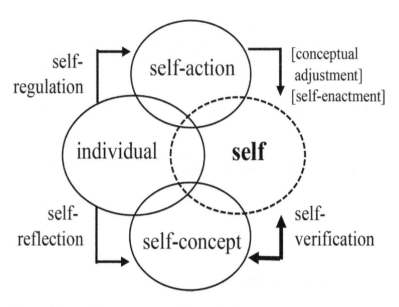

Figure 3.1   The structure of the self-phenomenon

As illustrated in Figure 3.1, the self is differentiated from the individual, self-concept, and self-action, albeit they are all interrelated. *The self is an entity that the individual (a) perceives to be their own existence and (b) seeks to regulate or enact as such.* The dotted-line circle, which represents the emic self, symbolizes the dual nature of self, and the size of the area in which the dotted-line circle overlaps the solid-line circle, which represents the individual, indicates the extent to which the individual understands and has control over their empirical existence, a measure of the *"selfing"* of one's existence.[27] The self-phenomenon is therefore a psychosocial process of self-engagement in which the individual identifies, evaluates, maintains, and transforms their existence in society. This combination of multiple components constitutes "a set of interrelated, functionally independent systems interacting in complex ways" (Morf and Mischel 2012: 25).[28] The remainder of the chapter examines in turn each of the four major constituents of the self-phenomenon and the relationships among them: the individual's *empirical existence, self-concept, self-action,* and *self.*

3.3.1 Empirical existence of the individual

The empirical existence of the individual in society is the foundation upon which the emic self of the individual rests. Humans are social beings, and it is in association with others that humans develop their selves, individuality, and personal identity. The empirical existence of the individual as a member of society comprises five parts: *corporeal, material, social, spiritual, and behavioral.*[29] The *corporeal* part consists of the biological body of the individual. The primordial needs (e.g., for food and sex) and the carnal feelings (e.g., pain and pleasure) and emotions (e.g., joy, fear, and anger) that come with the biological body supply the primitive drive and motivation for the "self-seeking" of the individual.[30] This primitive drive is channeled culturally in society and turned into an internal force for social action. Other aspects of the body, such as skin color, body shape, and physical strength are culturally symbolized as well, although the individual may not be fully aware of the cultural dimension of their corporality.[31] The corporeal part of the individual's empirical existence also consists of the unique mental capacities that human species are endowed with by nature, among which the capacities for self-reflection and self-regulation are crucial for the development of the self. Last but not least, the biological body has a finite lifespan, a temporal succession of activities that has a certain trajectory and an ending point.

The *material* part of the individual's empirical existence consists of the material objects that society regards as belonging to the individual. Those objects range from personal items such as clothing, bags, and cell phones to real estate properties such as land, houses, and businesses. The relationship between the individual and such material objects is determined by the ownership laws, conventions, and practices of the society in which the individual lives, regardless of the individual's knowledge of the actual ownership status of the objects. Children, for example, may play with toys without knowing that these toys are not theirs, and a person in a coma may be treated at a hospital they own but may be unaware of their ownership at the time due to the coma. There is also a gray area between the corporeal and material parts of the individual's empirical existence. Pacemakers, artificial limbs, and dental implants are material objects that become essential for the functioning of the biological bodies of their users.

The *social* part of the individual's empirical existence is composed of the individual's social networks as well as the individual's social standing within the networks. *Social networks* consist of people with whom the individual is associated based on birth, residence, profession, and other factors, and they include the individual's parents, siblings, neighbors, coworkers, friends, online and offline acquaintances, and so on. *Social standing* refers to the individual's position within a network ranked in terms of power, wealth, reputation, and the like. The combination of the individual's social networks and social standing constitutes the individual's social capital as well as potential sources of social conflict. It needs to be pointed out that the individuals do not have full knowledge of their social networks nor how others in the networks perceive and act toward them.

The *spiritual* part of the individual's empirical existence pertains to the psychological characteristics of the individual, such as the individual's temperament, personality, beliefs, and values. Although this is essentially a subjective and private domain, one can be blind to one's own psychological conditions without self-examination and self-reflection.

Finally, the *behavioral* part of the individual's empirical existence includes all the activities – verbal or physical – the individual was ever engaged in and the ways in which the individual conducted these activities. The activities may have been directed at humans or nonhumans, and may have been instinctual, habitual, or calculative. Unless they are self-consciously examined by the individual, those activities remain hidden from or incomprehensible to the individual.

The empirical existence of the individual, therefore, is a first-order object, i.e., an object that exists in itself or as it is. One comes into existence through birth before gaining self-awareness; as self-awareness grows, one begins to claim parts of one's empirical existence as one's own by declaring them to be "me" or "mine." *The claimed portion of one's empirical existence becomes one's emic self.* However, one may misperceive one's empirical existence and make mistakes in self-declarations, e.g., failing to recognize certain parts of one's own existence or claiming the parts of the existence as one's own that belong to others. For this reason, it has been argued that the empirical existence of an individual can be known in its entirety only by an omniscient being, if there is one, who by definition knows everything objectively. For example, Owen Flanagan (1991),[32] a philosopher, describes the total empirical existence of an individual as the "actual full identity" of the individual which he argues will come to be known with clarity and accuracy only on Judgment Day.

3.3.2 Self-concept

The second major component of the self-phenomenon is the self-concept of the individual. Endowed with the capacity for self-reflection, human individuals come to possess a mental representation of their empirical existence through self-perception and self-evaluation. This mental image of oneself that one has is one's *self-concept*,[33] which includes three aspects: *cognitive, evaluative,* and *affective.* The *cognitive* aspect pertains to the *self-identity* of the individual that defines and demarcates "me" or "mine." One's self-identity can be situational and transient (e.g., "I'm an audience at this theater") or general and enduring (e.g., "I'm a person with a good heart"). In essence, however, self-identity locates the position of the individual within society and specifies the role the individual is supposed to play in that position.[34] Because the individual is situated in different domains of social life, the same individual will have multiple identities. For instance, a person may be a college student, a music tutor, and a part-time worker at a local coffee shop; each of these positions and roles carries a specific set of expectations and responsibilities. Depending on the situation the individual is in, the different self-identities the individual has may cause multiple "person–role conflicts" (Turner 1970).[35] Self-identity also has a temporal dimension – the identification of the individual's past, present, and future. A person's self-identity for the future includes what Markus and Nurius (1986)[36] call a "possible self," i.e., one's belief about what one can become, would like to become, or is afraid of becoming. In sum, self-identity is what one thinks one was, is, will and can possibly be.

Self-identity is intrinsically self-evaluative. The *evaluative* aspect of self-concept involves the individual's effort to assess one's standing in society relative to those of others. Society is the cooperation among competing individuals who, among other things, fight for distinction and recognition.[37] While the criteria for success are socially constructed, they are internalized as the self-values of the individual which become the standards for the individual's self-evaluation. *Self-values* are biographically formed, influenced by the life experience of the individual in interacting with others. Values are enduring beliefs about what constitutes the desirable or preferable in life,[38] and self-values are "conceptions of the desirable which serve as standards or criteria for self-judgment" (Rosenberg 1979: 18).[39] Self-values are therefore a critical component of self-concept, for they add valence to one's self-identity. For example, whether one considers oneself to be too heavy or not is not so much an issue of how much one actually weighs as the issue of how much one thinks one ideally should weigh. Likewise, whether getting a grade of a "B" for a course is good enough or not largely depends on how much importance one attaches to that course and, perhaps, to grades in general. If self-identity is to locate where one is in society, self-values are the moral compass that prescribes what and where one should or ought to be.

Self-evaluation directly impacts the *affective* aspect of self-concept which consists of self-conscious emotions or *self-emotions* for short. Emotion is a form of affect involving both physiological and cognitive responses. Not all human emotions are self-conscious emotions, though. A person may feel pleased looking out the window seeing that the sun is shining and the flowers are blooming, but that positive feeling has nothing to do with the person's self-concept. *Self-conscious emotions* are a subset of personal affect that pertains to how individuals feel about themselves as a result of their self-evaluation.[40] Such self-emotions are evoked when individuals judge themselves to have lived up to or failed to live up to the standards that they set for themselves. Depending on the valence – positive or negative – of the emotions that self-evaluation generates and whether the individuals believe they are responsible for the failure or success of meeting their self-standards, four distinct types of self-conscious emotions can be differentiated: (1) positive or (2) negative feelings about oneself for things that one holds oneself responsible for (e.g., pride or shame), and (3) positive or (4) negative feelings about oneself for things that one does not hold oneself responsible for (e.g., self-satisfaction or self-disappointment).[41] The ability to reflect on one's existence and evaluate oneself according to one's self-standards is a necessary condition for the emergence of self-conscious emotions.

While it is a mental representation of one's empirical existence, self-concept is never an exact photocopy of that existence; rather, it is a *partial, selective,* and *biased* representation. Self-concept is a *partial* representation of one's empirical existence because no individuals are able to perceive the entirety of their existence. One learns about the early years of one's life, for example, from one's parents; one does not know for sure one's reputation in the eyes of others; and there are many other "blind spots" in one's life that one is unaware of (e.g., the hidden talents one possesses). Self-concept is also a *selective* representation of one's empirical existence because one is more interested in aspects of one's life that one deems important and less interested in what one regards as insignificant or trivial. Hence, trendy persons pay closer attention to the clothing they wear, and foodie people are pickier about the food they eat. Finally, self-concept is a *biased* representation of one's empirical existence because one's view of oneself is always tinted with the "*egocentric biases*" inherent in an emic perspective. Examples of such biases are the "self-serving attribution,"[42] i.e., the tendency to credit one's successes to internal abilities and blame external factors for one's failures, and the "self-defensive attribution,"[43] which is the attempt to explain one's mishaps in a way that minimizes a perceived threat to oneself. Those attributes of the mental representations of one's existence make self-concept function much like a moving spotlight that shines only on the part of one's empirical existence one deems relevant and important.

3.3.3   Self-action

The third component of the self-phenomenon is the self-conscious action taken by the individual. In tandem with the capacity for self-reflection, human individuals are also endowed with the capacity for conscious *self-regulation*, i.e., "the exercise of control over oneself, especially with regard to bringing the self into line with preferred (thus, regular) standards" (Vohs and Baumeister 2004: 2).[44] Many organisms are capable of controlling their behavior in multiple ways – instinctual, habitual, and intuitive – but humans are able to regulate their behavior at the self-conscious level. Through rational thinking and moral reasoning, human individuals make plans for action and coordinate their collective activities for the achievement of common goals. Self-conscious actions are a subset of human self-regulation that involves the application of one's self-concept, particularly one's self-values, to what one intends to do. Self-conscious actions are, therefore, a form of *self-enactment*, i.e., the actualization of one's self-concept through one's self-conscious action.

In a way it can be argued that all human conscious activities are self-conscious in nature, for the self-interest of the individual is almost always implicated in the individual's conscious action. Depending on the extent to which one's self-concept is involved in one's activities, two subtypes of self-conscious action can be distinguished: *self-relevant* and *self-centric*. Not all human conscious behaviors are explicitly self-conscious.[45] The activity of solving a mathematic problem, for example, involves the application of mathematical theorems and formulas rather than one's self-concept, and thus such activities are not self-conscious actions in the strict sense. However, those activities are *self-relevant* because their outcomes have implications for one's self-concept. In *self-centric* conscious actions, on the other hand, self-concept becomes a salient factor that directly influences one's conscious activities. The main function of such actions is to manage one's position in society and one's relationship with others. Examples of self-centric conscious action include *impression management, position management,* and *collaboration management.*

Impression management is one's self-presentation in the presence of others. As Goffman (1959: 4) points out, "when an individual appears in the presence of others, there will usually be some reason for him to mobilize his activity so that it will convey an impression to others which it is in his interests to convey."[46] The public persona of an individual belongs to this realm, for the persona is the impression of oneself the individual would like others to have which is created and maintained by the individual through dramaturgical performance. According to Goffman, dramaturgical performance takes place in the "front stage" where audiences are present through the expressions the individual *gives* (i.e., messages given at the face value of the expressions) as well as the expressions the individual *gives off* (i.e., messages implied or hinted at by the given expressions).[47] Preparations for impression management, however, occur in the "backstage" away from the audience, where individuals engage in activities like grooming, dressing up, and rehearsal.

Position management involves the efforts to maintain or alter one's current standing or relationship in society. In a certain sense, impression management can also be seen as a form of position management because one's public persona contributes to one's social standing, but position management is more than dramaturgical performance. The positions individuals occupy in society are determined by their access to such factors as power, wealth, and status; therefore, attempts to change any of those factors constitute position management. Such activities involve the application of one's self-concept and are guided by one's self-values. Interpersonal gift-giving, party-throwing, bad-mouthing others, or infighting are all examples of self-conscious actions for position management. Position management, however, may also be implicit in activities that involve no direct or immediate positional exchange or confrontation with others. For instance, pursuing a higher education increases the probability of obtaining a certain type of job after graduation, which can in turn change one's social position and the trajectory of one's life path.

Collaboration management refers to cooperation among individuals for the accomplishment of a common goal. Cooperative activities involve "the fitting together of the lines of behavior of the separate participants" (Blumer 1969: 70),[48] and such joint actions require participating individuals to communicate their intentions and expectations to others, to bring their actions in line with the established mutual expectations, and to make corrective adjustments whenever needed. Cooperative activities are also found in animal societies where the individuals lack self-consciousness, such as communal brood care in ant colonies and cooperative hunting in wolf packs. Those collaborative activities are mostly controlled by genetically programmed "operation manuals" (Holldobler and Wilson 2009)[49] and behavioral patterns imprinted on the individuals in the early stage of life.[50] As such, the mode of operation is rigid and difficult to change. Human self-conscious collaboration management, on the other hand, is highly flexible, and more responsive to situational variations. Through self-monitoring and mutual adjustment of intentions and activities, humans are able to cooperate at different levels in different situations, ranging from dyadic relationship, group interaction, to collaborations among nation-states.

Self-conscious actions, either self-relevant or self-centric, are activities that involve the awareness of not only one's own goals and interests but those of others as well. Being self-conscious in one's action therefore also implies being sensitive to the needs and expectations of others, and such sensitivity makes individuals mindful of the social repercussions and moral implications of the actions they take. However, in some situations a certain level of "no self"[51] in the conscious activities of the individuals might be desirable for promoting spontaneity and authenticity as in the case of "dancing like no one is watching" and "singing like no one is listening."

3.3.4   The self

The fourth major component of the self-phenomenon is the *self proper*, which is the entity that one takes to be oneself. To understand the self as an emic object, it is essential to differentiate the self from the empirical existence of the individual on the one hand and the self-concept of the individual on the other, as McIntosh (1995: 15–16) remarks:

> Not only is the self not to be equated with the lifeworld person, but also it should not be equated with a self-image or self-representation as is so often done … When I think about myself, have feelings about myself, look at myself, what I am thinking about, having feelings about, and perceiving is not an image or representation of anything, but quite simply a person, my own person seen from my own perspective, as distinct from the lifeworld perspective.[52]

"The lifeworld person" is similar in connotation to the empirical existence of the individual and the "lifeworld perspective" to the etic perspective. The first-order empirical existence of an individual can be perceived etically by others from outside and emically by the individual from within. It is the emically perceived own existence of the individual that constitutes the individual's *self*, namely, *the empirical existence one perceives to be one's own*. The self is thus a second-order object. The self is the *perceived* empirical existence, rather than the empirical existence per se; it is the empirical existence perceived *by oneself*, rather than by others; and it is the empirical existence perceived by oneself *as one's own*, rather than as someone else's. This conception of self can be further explicated by focusing on the *attributes*, *composition*, and *temporality* of the emic object.

Four *attributes* of the self are particularly important. First, *the self is an emic perception of one's empirical existence*. One's perceived own existence differs from one's actual empirical existence in that one's perception is influenced not just by the characteristics of one's empirical existence but also by the characteristics of one's perceptual apparatus, including one's egocentric biases.[53] For example, what your friends actually think of you belongs to your empirical existence, but what *you* think your friends think of you becomes part of your perceived own existence, i.e., your emic self. Your perception of yourself can be inaccurate because your friends may refrain from telling you what they really think of you in fear that the truth may hurt your feelings, and also because your own self-esteem may prevent you from knowing the truth about yourself. As a result, others may have a more accurate view of you than you do yourself. Needless to say, one does have privileged access to many aspects of one's empirical existence, including one's thoughts and feelings, but one does not have firsthand knowledge of all aspects of one's own life.

Second, *the self is evoked by the moving spotlight of one's self-concept.* No individuals are capable of perceiving the entirety of their empirical existence all at once. At any given time, only a small portion of one's empirical existence is accessible to one's perceptual experience, and the part of one's existence highlighted by one's self-concept becomes the self that one focuses on at the given moment. When you look at yourself in the mirror, for instance, you see the front of your body, particularly your face; when you turn sideway, you see a side of your body. Likewise, when you text another person, you focus on what you type on the cell phone. In each case, only a portion of your perceptual experience becomes figure, and the rest of it becomes the ground. As the focus of your attention shifts, your perception of your own existence changes accordingly. Self-exploration and self-discovery are the processes through which individuals come to gain knowledge and understanding of themselves that they did not have before.

Third, *one's self may not correspond to one's empirical existence.* Normally, one's perceptions of oneself are more or less in line with one's empirical existence, egocentric biases aside. However, it is possible that individuals may misperceive their own existence such that their self-perceptions become illusions or even delusions. For example, one may consider oneself to be highly popular among one's friends, but in fact the opposite is true. The difference between self-illusion and self-delusion lies in the fact that while self-illusion is caused by misleading or misinterpreted perceptual data, self-delusion is caused by false beliefs in the absence of any credible perceptual information. Mistaking one's chest pain for a heart attack is a self-illusion but misbelieving that one has literally lost one's heart is a self-delusion. Sometimes, however, the distinction between normal and pathological self-perceptions is difficult to draw, and it is therefore wise to always maintain a certain degree of self-doubt and double-check one's perceptions of one's own existence.

Fourth, *self is not self-concept.* Self-concept is a mental representation of one's empirical existence, and this mental image of oneself enables one to recognize oneself when one sees it. In this sense, one cannot have a self without having a self-concept. However, the self contains an empirical dimension that self-concept lacks. For example, when one raises one's lower arms and sees two hands, one knows they are one's own hands and one feels pain if they are pinched. The perceived hands are part of one's self. Apart from the actual hands one sees and feels, one also has a mental representation of what one's hands look and feel like, and that image one carries in one's head is part of one's self-concept. One's self and self-concept normally match, but discrepancies can occur. Suppose that a person had a tragic auto accident and lost one arm. After waking up from a drug-induced coma, the patient is horrified to discover that one arm is missing. This is an instance in which a person's self-perception (e.g., "my arm is missing") is at odds with the person's self-concept (e.g., "I should have two arms").

When a discrepancy between self and self-concept occurs, the individual will try hard to resolve it. The individual will either alter self-concept to make it match self or change self to make it conform to self-concept. In the case of the missing arm, the person will eventually have to accept a new self-concept that fits the changed self. Modification of out-dated self-concepts to reflect new self-perceptions is a common way in which individuals adapt themselves to the changing social environment. Surrounded by loving caregivers, for example, young children tend to have an overly positive view of themselves,[54] but this rosy self-concept will sooner or later be replaced with a more realistic one when young children grow into adolescence and their lifeworld expands to include competitive peers and other less patronizing people. To understand the constitution of the self, it is therefore necessary to examine not only the self-concept of the individual, but, more importantly, also the social environment in which the self is embedded.

The *composition* of the self of the individual corresponds more or less to the composition of the individual's empirical existence. There are five constituent parts in the empirical existence of an individual: corporeal, material, social, spiritual, and behavioral, but the content of the self of an individual is not identical to that of the individual's empirical existence, for, as James (1918 [1890])[55] points out, only those that the individual comes to recognize as "me" or "mine" constitute the individual's self. "*Me*" is the totality of what the individual calls "*mine*." In theory, there should be five parts of "mine" in the self that correspond to the five parts of the individual's empirical existence. The *corporeal part* includes everything one calls "mine" when it comes to one's body: "my head," "my nose," "my chest," "my feet," etc. One usually pays most attention to one's face because it is the most recognizable aspect of one's body. The corporeal part of one's self also includes what Goffman (1959)[56] refers to as the "personal front," which consists of one's clothing, posture, gesture, voice, and the like, as these personal items follow one's body wherever it goes.

The other parts of one's self correspond to the remaining four constituent parts of one's empirical existence: the *material part* includes everything one calls "my possessions" or "my property"; the *social part* includes what one calls "my family," "my friends," "my reputation," and so on; the *spiritual part* consists of what one calls "my personality," "my beliefs," "my values," and other mental attributes one regards as "mine"; finally, the *behavioral part* includes those activities one believes that one is or was involved in. However, what specific elements there are in each part of the self and how much importance the individual attaches to them depend on many factors, including the life experience the individual has undergone.

The self of the individual also has a *temporal* dimension, which pertains to the change that occurs over time in the individual's perceived own existence. The trajectory of the temporal change in one's self more or less reflects the changes in one's empirical existence. Mirror self-recognition, for example, typically emerges around 18 months of age, and the understanding of "false beliefs" is usually achieved around 4 to 5 years of age.[57] As one's capacity for self-reflection grows and one's lifeworld expands, one's perceived own existence changes accordingly. For example, young children are more interested in their toys, adolescents pay more attention to their popularity among peers, and adults attach more importance to their career and family. One's past is stored in one's memory, retrieved to interpret one's current situation as well as the prospects for the future, and reconstituted in light of the new experiences one gains.[58] Therefore, one's perception and understanding of one's own existence is shaped by one's biographical experience which unfolds in a larger social arena, and as one's biographical experience changes, so does one's self.

3.4   Self-directed feedback system

Psychologists Morf and Mischel (2012: 22) describe the self as "a psycho-social dynamic processing system," through which "the person experiences the social, interpersonal world and interacts with it in characteristic self-guided ways, in a process of continuous self-construction and adaptation."[59] This dynamic system comprises not just the self proper but also other components of the self-phenomenon, which together constitute a self-guided feedback system, allowing individuals to consciously direct their engagement with the social world.

As shown in Figure 3.1, the starting point of the self-directed feedback system is the empirical existence of the individual embedded in society. The empirical existence of the individual comes into being the moment the individual was born. The endowed capacity for self-reflection develops in the early years of the individual's life through interaction of the individual with other members of society – mostly the caregivers. Around 4–5 years of age, the individual is able to take the perspectives of significant others and use them to examine and evaluate their own existence, leading to the formation of a narrative self-concept. The possession of the narrative self-concept enables the individual to identify and articulate their situatedness in society, thereby turning a portion of their empirical existence into perceived own existence, i.e., the self. As a member of the human species, the individual is also equipped with the capacity for self-regulation, which develops over time as the individual becomes physically and socially more mature. This ability allows the individual to engage in self-conscious action, aiming to construct, maintain, and alter one's relationship with others and, consequently, one's position in society.

A key link in the feedback system of the self-phenomenon is the process of *self-verification* – efforts made by the individual to maintain a correspondence between self-concept and self. Self-concept, once formed, acts like a roadmap that guides the individual's self-perception, and the individual is internally motivated to make sure that what one perceives oneself to be matches what one believes one is.[60] Seeing and believing affect each other: although believing influences seeing, seeing also changes believing. If a discrepancy between the two is found in self-verification, the individual will strive to eliminate the perceived mismatch by means of either *conceptual adjustment* or *self-enactment*, a self-guided process that "embodies characteristics of feedback control" (Carver 2004: 13).[61]

3.4.1   Conceptual adjustment

The process of self-verification begins with self-assessment. Self-conscious individuals constantly monitor and evaluate their existence in the social world, assessing the need for conceptual adjustment or self-enactment. As discussed previously, discrepancies between self-concept and self can occur due to changes in one's empirical existence. As a large part of one's empirical existence is not directly under the radar of one's perceptual surveillance, individuals tend to miss the early signs of change in their empirical existence. The onset of puberty, for example, takes place unnoticed initially until bodily changes become so salient that it is no longer possible for the individual to miss them. The moment one becomes aware of the change in one's empirical existence, one's perceived own existence is altered, causing a discordance between one's self-concept and self.

The occurrence of such a discordance will initially lead to an *interpretive adjustment* response by the individual, which is the effort to interpret the noticeable change in the perceived own existence in a way that it falls in line with one's existing self-concept. In other words, it is an attempt to explain away the uncovered inconsistency. For example, a student with a self-concept of high academic competency may explain the receipt of a low grade on an important exam in terms of lack of preparation, physical illness, or other external factors, characteristic of the manifestation of the attributional bias. So long as this type of interpretive adjustment works, the individual succeeds in maintaining a consistent and stable self-concept.

However, if interpretive adjustment fails to remove the discovered discrepancy between self-concept and self, the individual will resort to one of the two main strategies of self-verification: conceptual adjustment and self-enactment. *Conceptual adjustment* is the effort to change one's self-concept so that it matches one's perceived own existence. After repeated failures to receive top grades, for example, the over-confident student may finally come to the realization that "I'm probably not the smartest person in the class, but that's okay and I can accept that." In some instances, changes in one's perceived own existence may occur abruptly and drastically, e.g., the sudden loss of vision or mobility resulting from a serious accident or illness; such adverse occurrences will force the individual to undergo significant conceptual adjustment, which is often painful and depressing.[62] Successful conceptual adjustments restore the consistency between the individual's self-concept and self. Unresolved discrepancies in self-verification, on the other hand, can cause severe emotional disturbances such as the "identity crisis" in adolescents (Erikson 1959)[63] and the "midlife crisis" in adults (Neugarten 1968).[64]

3.4.2   Self-enactment

Discrepancies between self-concept and self can also occur due to changes in one's self-concept with no alteration in one's empirical existence. Such changes in self-concept could result from the individual's exposure to new ideas about life through watching a movie, reading a book, or having a conversation with another person. Such ideational exposures can cause individuals to reassess the ways they live and cause them to feel that their perceived own existence falls short of what they would like to be or what they think they ought to be. The opening of this perceptual gap in self-assessment may motivate a person to engage in *self-enactment* – the effort to change the empirical component of one's perceived own existence so that one's self-perception matches one's self-concept. The motivation to "act in according with the self-concept and to maintain it intact in the face of potentially challenging evidence" is also known as the "self-consistency" motive (Rosenberg 1986: 57).[65] But, in contrast to conceptual adjustment, which alters self-concept to make it reflect the change in the perceived own existence, self-enactment seeks to bring one's perceived own existence in line with one's self-concept by altering the empirical component of one's self-perception, i.e., one's empirical existence.

To enact one's self is therefore to actualize one's self-concept through self-conscious action. The actualization of one's self-concept involves the reshaping of one's perceived own existence by way of appropriating and modifying one's empirical existence. The process of altering one's empirical existence is simultaneously a process of expanding the scope of one's self-awareness and deepening the level of one's self-understanding, turning previously unknown elements of one's empirical existence into part of one's emic self. Working on a college degree, pursuing a career, forming a family, or becoming a parent are examples of self-enactment in which individuals put their personal plans and goals into action, reconstructing their lifeworld while at the same time increasing their self-knowledge. Self-enactment may also come as a reaction to the discovery of undesired changes in one's empirical existence. After receiving poor grades in a number of exams, for instance, a student may decide to redouble efforts to improve performance on tests rather than change self-concept by lowering self-standards. If the student is able to hold on to their self-concept by getting better grades on subsequent tests, the student succeeds in self-enactment; otherwise, the student will have to resort to conceptual adjustment by lowering self-expectations so that their self-concept falls in line with the perceived own existence.

Thus, to enact the self is to actualize what one wants to be, to adhere to one's self-standards in one's conduct, and to be true to one's self-feelings. As such, the successfulness of self-enactment is measured not in terms of the *veracity* of self-knowledge, i.e., the accuracy in the perception of one's empirical existence, but rather in terms of the imagination of a possible self that one aspires to have and the efficacy of one's effort to actualize it. In this sense, the self is not something to be found, but something to be envisioned and created. Success or failure in self-enactment will produce different self-conscious emotions: pride and high self-esteem in the case of success, and mortification and lower self-esteem in the case of failure. However, as James (1918 [1890])[66] aptly put it using the formula of achievement over self-expectation, self-esteem is a function of the mediation of one's actual accomplishment by one's aspirations: wise is the person who knows how to strike a balance between the two.

Finally, self-enactment has a moral dimension. As the self is socially embedded, any change made to one's empirical existence in society has potential implications for the lives of other social members. And the more efficacious one is in self-enactment, the bigger the impact the change in one's self will have on the lives of others. For this reason, the issue of self-enactment is as much about what one can be and wants to be as what one should or ought to be. Certainly, one cannot be held entirely responsible for what one was, is, and is to be, for a considerable part of one's empirical existence is ascribed rather than achieved. For instance, one did not choose one's biological parents, one's physical attributes, and one's early life experiences. In some societies, one's spouse, job, and residential place are all determined by others for oneself. Nevertheless, one always has a role to play in enacting one's self and affecting one's relationship with others no matter in what society one's life is embedded.

3.4.3   Iteration of self-verification

The striving of the individual for self-verification turns the self-phenomenon into a dynamic feedback system. The system consists of two distinct but related feedback loops: the loop of conceptual adjustment and the loop of self-enactment. Both loops start with the capacity for self-reflection that humans are endowed with, and this capacity enables individuals to form self-concepts that represent their perceived own existence. The process of self-reflection also keeps the individual constantly monitoring the linkage between self-concept and self to make sure that they match. When a discrepancy is found and cannot be eliminated through the initial effort of interpretive adjustment, the individual will activate either the *loop of conceptual adjustment* which changes the self-concept to make it correspond to the perceived own existence or the *loop of self-enactment* which alters the perceived own existence to make it conform to the self-concept. The activation of either loop is done through self-conscious action enabled by the endowed capacity for self-regulation. Both feedback loops aim to maintain a correspondence between self-concept and self through self-verification.

Self-verification is an iterative process. The concordance between self-concept and the perceived own existence is maintained, broken, restored, and broken again as one's engagement with society expands and deepens. The outcome of one round of self-verification becomes the input of the next round, and this iterative process continues throughout one's life. Through this process, individuals gain more knowledge of, and control over, their empirical existence in society. At the beginning, the individual's existence in the world is in an "in-itself" state, i.e., an existence without self-consciousness; gradually, the individual enters into a state of "for-itself" existence, in which the individual obtains a higher level of self-knowledge and self-control.[67] The continuous expansion of the scope of self-knowledge and self-control in the different realms of one's empirical existence constitutes the process of *"selfization"* – a process of turning the non-reflective "in-itself" state of one's existence into a self-conscious "for-itself" state of existence. As the psychiatrist Rogers (1951)[68] notes, at any given moment in time only a small portion of one's empirical existence is consciously experienced and recognized by oneself as one's own, although a much larger portion of it is accessible to self-consciousness. The iterative process of self-verification is an endless voyage of self-exploration and self-discovery, enabling individuals to travel farther and deeper into the unknown territories of their empirical existence in society: what was hidden before comes to light and what seemed to be impossible becomes within reach.

3.5   Conclusion

The self has been defined in this chapter as an emic object – what one takes to be one's own existence. The self is a part of the self-phenomenon that consists of three other components: the empirical existence of the individual, self-concept, and self-action. As the perceived own existence of the individual, the self is connected to the empirical existence of the individual through self-concept and self-action, and this connection involves three psychosocial processes – self-reflection, self-regulation, and self-verification. Together, they form a self-directed feedback system that enables individuals to become more self-conscious and have more control over their existence in society. Through the iterative processes of conceptual adjustment and self-enactment, individuals increasingly "selfize" their empirical existence in society, transforming the "in-itself" state of their existence into a more self-conscious state of "for-itself" existence.

Given that the self is the entity one perceives and acts toward as one's own existence, what then determines one's self-perception and self-conscious action? Why do individuals perceive and act toward themselves in different ways? Certainly, numerous factors are involved in influencing an individual's self-perception and self-action, but sociologists are primarily interested in the social determinants of the self. The questions that sociologists ask are: Why do individuals from different societies and cultures tend to perceive themselves in different ways? Why do individuals from different segments of society tend to have different selves? Such differences cannot be adequately accounted for by looking at the variations in individual characteristics. The next chapter examines some of the major social factors and mechanisms that shape the self of the individual, focusing in particular on their impacts on the formation of self-concept and the efficacy of an individual's self-action.

Notes

1. Mark R. Leary and June Price Tangney (2012) 'The self as an organizing construct in the behavioral and social sciences,' in M. R. Leary and J. P. Tangney (eds.), *Handbook of Self and Identity*. New York: The Guilford Press, pp. 1–18.
2. Dan Zahavi (2002) 'First-person thoughts and embodied self-awareness: Some reflections on the relation between recent analytical philosophy and phenomenology,' *Phenomenology and the Cognitive Sciences*, 1, 7–26.
3. Eric Olson (1998) 'There is no problem of the self,' *Journal of Consciousness Studies*, 5, 645–657.
4. Ulric Neisser (1988) 'Five kinds of self-knowledge,' *Philosophical Psychology*, 1, 35–59.
5. Peter Callero (2003) 'The sociology of the self,' *Annual Review of Sociology*, 29, 115–153.
6. Mark R. Leary and June Price Tangney (2012).
7. Roy F. Baumeister and Kathleen D. Vohs (2012) 'Self-regulation and the executive function of the self,' in M. R. Leary and J. P. Tangney (eds.), *Handbook of Self and Identity*. New York: The Guilford Press, pp. 180–197.
8. Charles S. Carver and Michael F. Scheier (1998) *On the Self-regulation of Behavior*. New York: Cambridge University Press.
9. Stanley B. Klein (2012) 'The two selves: The self of conscious experience and its brain,' in M. R. Leary and J. P. Tangney (eds.), *Handbook of Self and Identity*. New York: The Guilford Press, pp. 617–637.
10. Victor Gecas (1982) 'The self-concept,' *Annual Review of Sociology*, 8, 1–33.
11. Morris Rosenberg (1986) *Conceiving the Self*. Malabar, FL: Robert E. Krieger.
12. Karen A. Cerulo (1997) 'Identity construction: New issues, new directions,' *Annual Review of Sociology*, 23, 385–409.
13. Erving Goffman (1959) *The Presentation of Self in Everyday Life*. New York: Doubleday.
14. Jerome Bruner (2003) 'Self-making narratives,' in R. Fivush and C. A. Haden (eds.), *Autobiographical Memory and the Construction of a Narrative Self: Development and Cultural Perspectives*. Hillsdale, NJ: Lawrence Erlbaum Associates, pp. 209–225.
15. Jerrold Seigel (2005) *The Idea of the Self: Thought and Experience in Western Europe Since the Seventeenth Century*. Cambridge: Cambridge University Press.
16. George H. Mead (1934) *Mind, Self, and Society: From the Standpoint of a Social Behaviorist*. Chicago: The University of Chicago Press.
17. Herbert Blumer (1969) *Symbolic Interactionism: Perspective and Method*. Berkeley: The University of California Press.
18. Shanyang Zhao (2014) 'Self as an emic object: A re-reading of William James on self,' *Theory & Psychology*, 24(2), 199–216.
19. Shanyang Zhao (2017) "Self as a second-order object: Reinterpreting the Jamesian 'me'," *New Ideas in Psychology*, 46, 8–16.
20. "Etic" and "emic" were coined by Kenneth Pike from the suffixes of the words phonetic and phonemic. See Kenneth Pike (ed.) (1967) *Language in*

Relation to a Unified Theory of Structure of Human Behavior. The Hague: Mouton.

21. Marvin Harris (1976) 'History and significance of the emic/etic discussion,' *Annual Review of Anthropology,* 5, 329–350.

22. John Barresi and Chris Moore (1996) 'Intentional relations and social understanding,' *Behavioral and Brain Sciences,* 19, 107–154.

23. Dan Zahavi (2002).

24. Stanton Wortham (2000) 'Interactional positioning and narrative self-construction,' *Narrative Inquiry,* 10, 157–184.

25. Susan Harter (1999) *The Construction of the Self: A Developmental Perspective.* New York: Guilford.

26. In the literature, the self is sometimes dichotomized into the "I-self" and the "me-self" (see chapter 3 in Chad Gordon and Kenneth Gergen [eds.] [1968] *The Self in Social Interaction.* New York: John Wiley and Sons), which dates back to William James. This categorization fails to differentiate the emic self (i.e., "me") from the first-person singular perspective (i.e., "I"). The "I" is the reflectivity of the individual, and the emic self is what the reflective individual calls "me." See William James (1918 [1890]) *The Principles of Psychology* (Vol. 2). New York: Dover.

27. The term "selfing" was introduced by McAdams (1997: 56) in discussing James's concept of the "I": "The I is not a thing. Nor is it a part, a piece, a component, or even a facet of the self. The I is rather the process of being a self – a process we give the label *selfing.*" Dan McAdams (1997) 'The case for unity in the (post)modern self: A modest proposal,' in R. D. Ashmore and L. Jussim (eds.), *Self and Identity: Fundamental Issues.* New York: Oxford University Press, pp. 46–78.

28. Carolyn C. Morf and Walter Mischel (2012) 'The self as a psycho-social dynamic processing system: Toward a Converging Science of Selfhood,' in M. R. Leary and J. P. Tangney (eds.), *Handbook of Self and Identity.* New York: The Guilford Press, pp. 21–49.

29. This classification is derived from the one suggested by William James that divided the empirical existence of the individual into three parts: material, social, and spiritual. See William James (1918 [1890]).

30. Ibid.

31. See Maurice Merleau-Ponty (1958 [1945]) *Phenomenology of Perception.* Tr. Colin Smith. London: Routledge.

32. Owen Flanagan (1991) *Varieties of Moral Personality.* Cambridge, MA: Harvard University Press.

33. Also known as "self-schema" in psychology. See Hazel Markus (1977) 'Self-schemata and processing information about the self,' *Journal of Personality and Social Psychology,* 35, 63–78.

34. See Sheldon Stryker (1980) *Symbolic Interactionism: A Social Structural Version.* Reading, MA: Benjamin.

35. Ralph H. Turner (1970) 'The role and the person,' *American Journal of Sociology,* 84, 1–23.

36. Hazel Rose Markus and Paula Nurius (1986) 'Possible selves,' *American Psychologist,* 41, 954–969.

37. Axel Honneth (2014) *The I in We: Studies in the Theory of Recognition.* Malden, MA: Polity.
38. Milton Rokeach (1973) *The Nature of Human Values.* New York: Free Press.
39. Morris Rosenberg (1979) *Conceiving the Self.* New York: Basic.
40. Michael Lewis (1995) 'Self-conscious emotions,' *American Scientist,* 83, 68–78.
41. Kristjan Kristjansson (2010) *The Self and Its Emotions.* Cambridge: Cambridge University Press.
42. Dale Miller and Michael Ross (1975) 'Self-serving biases in the attribution of causality: Fact or fiction?', *Psychological Bulletin,* 82, 213–225.
43. Jeff Greenberg (2007) 'Defensive attribution,' in R. F. Baumeister and K. D. Vohs (eds.), *Encyclopedia of Social Psychology.* Los Angeles: Sage, pp. 230–231.
44. Kathleen D. Vohs and Roy F. Baumeister (2004) 'Understanding self-regulation: An introduction,' in R. F. Baumeister and K. D. Vohs (eds.), *Handbook of Self-regulation: Research, Theory, and Application.* New York: The Guilford Press, pp. 1–12.
45. For a detailed philosophical discussion, see Raphael Milliere (2020) 'The varieties of selflessness,' *Philosophy and the Mind Sciences,* 1, 1–41.
46. Erving Goffman (1959).
47. Ibid.
48. Herbert Blumer (1969).
49. Bert Holldobler and Edward O. Wilson (2009) *The Super-Organism: The Beauty, Elegance, and Strangeness of Insect Societies.* New York: W. W. Norton.
50. David L. Mech (2003 [1970]) *The Wolf: The Ecology and Behavior of an Endangered Species.* Minneapolis: University of Minnesota Press.
51. See Peter Kaufman (2014) 'A sociology of no-self: Applying Buddhist social theory to symbolic interaction,' *Symbolic Interaction,* 37, 264–282.
52. Donald McIntosh (1995) *Self, Person, World: The Interplay of Conscious and Unconscious in Human Life.* Evanston, IL: Northwestern University Press.
53. Block (1999), for example, points out that there are two elements in the human perception of color: the objective color (actual color) and the subjective person-relative color (unique color) which is influenced by the individual's perceptual apparatus. See Ned Block (1999) 'Sexism, racism, ageism, and the nature of consciousness,' *Philosophical Topics,* 26(1/2), 39–71.
54. Susan Harter (1999).
55. In the early days, a number of sociologists used different first-person pronouns to refer to the different elements of the self-phenomenon. James used "I" to refer to self-reflectivity and "me" or "mine" to the self. Mead used "I" to refer to individual creativity and "me" to the internalized social values. Cooley abolished the "I-me" distinction and used "I," "me," "my," and "mine" interchangeably to refer to what he called the "social self." See Charles H. Cooley (1956 [1902]) 'Human nature and the social order,' in R. C. Angell (ed.), *The Two Major Works of Charles H. Cooley: Social Organization [and] Human Nature and the Social Order.* Glencoe, IL: Free Press, pp. 1–451; William James (1918 [1890]).
56. Erving Goffman (1959).

57. Michael Tomasello (2018) 'How children come to understand false beliefs: A shared intentionality account,' *PNAS*, 115, 8491–8498.
58. David H. Demo (1992) 'The self-concept over time: Research issues and directions,' *Annual Review of Sociology*, 18, 303–326.
59. Carolyn C. Morf and Walter Mischel (2012).
60. William B. Swann, Jr. and Stephen J. Read (1981) 'Self-verification processes: How we sustain our self-conceptions,' *Journal of Experimental Social Psychology*, 17, 351–372.
61. Charles S. Carver (2004) 'Self-regulation of action and affect,' in R. F. Baumeister and K. D. Vohs (eds.), *Handbook of Self-regulation: Research, Theory, and Applications*. New York: Guilford, pp. 13–39.
62. Anjali J. Forber-Pratt, Dominique A. Lyew, Carlyn Mueller, and Leah B. Samples (2017) 'Disability identity development: A systematic review of the literature,' *Rehabilitation Psychology*, 62(2), 198–207.
63. Erik Erikson (1959) 'The problem of ego-identity,' *Psychological Issue*, 1, 101–164.
64. Bernice L. Neugarten (1968) 'The awareness of middle age,' in B. L. Neugarten (ed.), *Middle Age and Aging*. Chicago: University of Chicago Press, pp. 93–98.
65. Morris Rosenberg (1986).
66. William James (1918 [1890]).
67. The terms of "being-in-itself" and "being-for-itself" were originally coined by Hegel to refer to two distinctive modes of existence. Basically, being-in-itself is existence without self-awareness and being-for-itself is existence with self-awareness. See G. W. F. Hegel (1977 [1807]) *Phenomenology of Spirit*, tr. A. V. Miller. Oxford: Oxford University Press.
68. Carl R. Rogers (1951) *Client-Centered Therapy: Its Current Practice, Implications, and Theory*. Boston, MA: Houghton Mifflin.

Further reading

Cooley, Charles H. (1956 [1902]) *Human Nature and the Social Order*, in R. C. Angell (ed. and intro.), *The Two Major Works of Charles H. Cooley: Social Organization [and] Human Nature and the Social Order*. Glencoe, IL: Free Press, pp. 1–451.
James, William (1918 [1890]) *The Principles of Psychology* (Vol. 2). New York: Dover.
Mead, George H. (1934) *Mind, Self, and Society: From the Standpoint of a Social Behaviorist*. Chicago: The University of Chicago Press.
Zhao, Shanyang (2017) 'Self as a second-order object: Reinterpreting the Jamesian "me",' *New Ideas in Psychology*, 46, 8–16.

4   Social determinants of the self

The self is an entity that the individual recognizes to be "me" or "mine" and reflects upon and acts toward as their own existence. However, there are differences within a society as well as across societies in the ways in which individuals perceive and act toward themselves. This chapter examines the *social factors* that shape the self of the individual, with a particular focus on the *mechanisms* by which the social factors influence the constitution and transformation of the self. For the purposes of the analysis that follows, a few conceptual clarifications are in order.

First, a distinction between neurocognitive and sociocultural factors needs to be made. *Neurocognitive* factors are the internal neurological and psychological conditions that provide the individual with the capabilities for self-reflection and self-regulation. Without such capabilities, there can be no reflective human self-awareness. *Sociocultural* factors, on the other hand, are interpersonal, institutional, and cultural characteristics of the society that provide the social contexts in which individuals engage in self-reflection and self-regulation. In the absence of such contexts, there can be no self even if the individual has the neurocognitive capacities for self-reflection and self-regulation. In this chapter, neurocognitive factors are called the *prerequisites* of the self and sociocultural factors the *determinants* of the self. Both types of factors are necessary for the constitution of the self, but the focus of analysis in this chapter is on the latter.

Second, a further distinction needs to be made between determinants and mechanisms. While *determinants* are causal factors that contribute to the outcome of interest, *mechanisms* are the processes by which causal factors produce the outcome of interest under given conditions. The given conditions are also described here as *domains of application* for the relevant causal mechanisms. Mere identification of determinants without knowing the underlying mechanisms is insufficient for understanding causal relationships; moreover, it is also important to specify the condition under which a given mechanism operates as no causal mechanism works under all conditions. "Significant others," for example, is a social determinant of the self, "reflected appraisal" is the mechanism by which significant others come to shape the self-concept of the individual, and the part of the individual's existence that resides in the "eyes of others" in the form of the individual's reputation and popularity constitutes the specific domain of application for reflected appraisal.

Third, attention will also be paid to the social determinants and causal mechanisms that affect *self-conscious action*. As has been explicated in the previous chapter, the self is more than a self-concept; rather, it is an entity that the individual perceives and acts toward as their own existence. The study of the self, therefore, needs to include the study of both self-concept and self-action.

4.1   Prerequisites of the self

The neurocognitive capacities of the individual for self-reflection and self-regulation and the sociocultural embedment of the individual are two fundamentally important prerequisites of the self. The former is a mental attribute of the human species, and the latter is a social attribute of the human individual. Both attributes are required for the formation of the self.

4.1.1   Neurocognitive capacities

Not all organisms possess the neural and cognitive requirements for acquiring the self. To have a self, an organism must have the capabilities for self-reflection and self-regulation. *Self-reflection* is the ability to become an object of one's own attention with the awareness that the object one attends to is one's own existence. Two levels of such *self-awareness* have been differentiated: perceptual self-awareness and conceptual self-awareness.[1] *Perceptual self-awareness* originates from the direct experience with one's own body and its sensory contact with the physical environment, such as bodily sensations and proprioception; *conceptual self-awareness*, on the other hand, involves information about one's mental states (e.g., beliefs, values, and attitudes) as well as one's relationships with others (e.g., popularity and reputation). While perceptual self-awareness might be found among animals, conceptual self-awareness is believed to be distinctively human.[2] The self of the human individual involves both perceptual and conceptual self-awareness.

The cognitive capacity for conceptual self-awareness is grounded in a *neural substrate* that enables the human individual to process symbolic information, particularly language. The use of language for communication with other members of society makes it possible for individuals to share mental states as well as conduct private "inner speech" (Morin 2011),[3] a condition that is indispensable for the emergence of conceptual self-awareness. The *prefrontal cortex* of the human brain has been identified as a critical region for self-inferential activities, and the *Broca's area*, also known as the left inferior frontal gyrus (LIFG), has been shown to be directly involved in language use.[4] In addition, the prefrontal cortex has been found to be the primary brain region responsible for *self-regulation*, particularly the executive function.[5] However, the exact neuroanatomic localization of self-reflection and self-regulation remains undetermined, for there is a possibility that the neural bases for self-inferential activities are located in multiple parts of the brain, rather than confined to a single region.[6]

Humans are endowed with the neurocognitive prerequisites of the self phylogenetically through natural evolution, and the capabilities for self-reflection and self-regulation develop ontogenetically in the early years of the individual's life. The individual's capability to have a self will be impaired if the required neurocognitive structures are undeveloped or damaged.

4.1.2 Sociocultural embedment

The possession of the endowed neurocognitive capacity for self-referential activities in itself is insufficient for the acquisition of the self, for the formation of the self also requires a sociocultural environment in which the individual interacts with other members of society. The embedment of the individual in society is a necessary condition for the acquisition of the self for three main reasons. First of all, the empirical existence of the individual in society is the foundation upon which the self of the individual rests. Although the empirical existence per se is not the self, there can be no self without it, and the way the individual is embedded in society affects the self-perception of the individual.

Second, the self is a product *for* social interaction. According to the German philosopher Hegel (1977 [1807]),[7] the self emerges for the purposes of aiding human competition for social recognition. To be successful in this competition, one needs to be aware of how others perceive and evaluate oneself, and the awareness of others' perceptions of oneself becomes one's self-awareness. In other words, the self-awareness of the individual is the individual's awareness of others' awareness of the individual.

Third, the self is not only a product for social interaction but also a product *of* social interaction. It is through interacting with others that one's self emerges. To become an object to oneself, as Blumer (1969: 13) explains, one must see oneself from the standpoint of others: "One can do this only by placing himself in the position of others and viewing himself or acting toward himself from that position."[8] The neurocognitive prerequisites human species possess provide human individuals with the capacities for self-reflection and self-regulation, but it is the embedment of the individual in society, i.e., interaction with others, that actualizes those capacities for the individual. In an environment of complete social isolation, one cannot have a self and does not need a self.

The actualization of the capability for possessing the self takes place in the early years of a person's life. Among other things, there is a "critical period" in childhood for language acquisition, during which time the neural system "awaits specific instructional information ... to continue to develop normally" (Knudsen 1999: 637).[9] Lack of verbal communication with other members of society during this critical period of time will cause irreversible damage to the development of a person's normal language ability and, consequently, the possession of the self.

4.1.3   Social schemas and social resources

Neurocognitive capacities and sociocultural embedment are the important prerequisites for the acquisition of the self, but in order to explain the variations in the selves possessed by individuals within and across societies it is necessary to examine the differences in the specific conditions under which the selves of individuals are constituted. Sociological research on the self seeks to understand the formation of self in terms of the characteristics of the society in which the individuals are embedded. *Social schemas* and *social resources* have been identified in the literature as two prominent structural features of human society.[10] The remainder of this chapter focuses on the impact of these two societal factors on the constitution of the self. Figure 4.1 depicts the causal pathways that link the different components of the self-phenomenon to the larger society through social schemas and social resources. As shown in the diagram, the empirical existence of the individual is an integral part of society, and the way in which the individual is embedded in society exposes the individual to certain types of social schemas that in turn influence the individual's self-concept, and the particular social embedment also makes available to the individual certain social resources for self-conscious action. The combination of these two structural pathways shapes the formation of the individual's self.

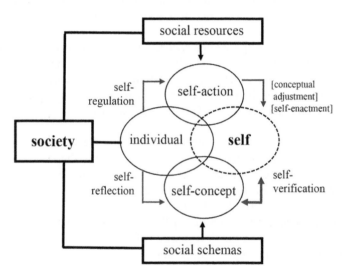

Figure 4.1   Social determinants of the self

4.2   Social schemas and self-concept

"Self reflects society" is a basic tenet of the sociological theory of the self.[11] Embedded in the sociocultural environment, the self of the individual is shaped by the structure of the society of which the individual is a member. *Rules* and *resources* are the two defining features of social structure,[12] and they impinge on the "internal dynamics of self-processes" to produce different types of personal identity (Stryker and Burke 2000: 285).[13] To understand the reflection of society in the self of the individual, it is necessary to examine how social rules and resources come to shape the constitution of the self.

As "generalizable procedures applied in the enactment/reproduction of social life" (Giddens 1984: 21),[14] rules can be divided into two types according to their level of codification: formal versus informal. *Formal rules* are statutes that are stipulated and enforced by institutional agencies, such as organizational regulations, state laws, and national constitutions; *informal rules*, on the other hand, are less codified ways of doing things, such as customs, etiquettes, form of address, recipes, and fashion. Because "informal rules" goes beyond what the word "rules" generally means, Sewell (1992: 8)[15] has argued that the concept "*social schemas*" can be used to refer to all types of generalizable procedures, formal or informal, in social life. Unlike rules that are often explicitly applied to organized activities, schemas can be implicit in virtually anything people do in social life: what they think, what they say, and how they act toward themselves and others.

As depicted in Figure 4.1, social schemas shape the self by shaping the self-concept of the individual. Self-concept, which consists of cognitive, evaluative, and affective dimensions, is the individual's mental representation of their empirical existence in society. In psychology, self-concept is also called "self-schemata" defined as cognitive generalizations about the self that "organize and guide the processing of self-related information contained in the individual's social experiences" (Markus 1977: 64).[16] Self-concept, therefore, doesn't only reflect the individual's embedment in society but also guides the individual's activities toward it. Sociologically, the challenge is to explain how social schemas, a structural factor of society, enter into the self-concept of the individual, that is, to specify the *mechanisms* by which social schemas shape the formation of self-concept.

Reflected appraisal, social comparison, and *cultural conditioning* are three primary social mechanisms that account for how social schemas influence the formation of self-concept. What lies at the core of the linkage between social schemas and self-concept is the conversion of the *social standards* of conduct into the *self-standards* of the individual. Such standards of conduct define for the individual how to behave and live properly as a member of society, and they are also used by others to evaluate the individual and by the individual to evaluate themselves. The transmission of the standards of conduct from the society to the individual essentially involves the following three steps: (a) the explication of the standards to the individual by social agents, (b) the incorporation of the social standards into the self-values of the individual, and (c) the application of the internalized social standards to the relevant aspects of the individual's existence. Depending on the differences in the characteristics of the social agents, the social standards, and the individual attributes being evaluated, different *social mechanisms of self-concept formation* come into play.

4.2.1   Reflected appraisal

Reflected appraisal is undoubtedly the most well-known social mechanism of self-concept formation in sociology and social psychology. The basic principle of reflected appraisal is that individuals' thoughts and feelings about themselves reflect the thoughts and feelings that others have about them. Cooley (1956 [1902])[17] popularized this principle by introducing the concept of the "looking-glass self" which describes the view individuals have of themselves as mirroring the attitudes of others toward them. Metaphorically, in other words, self-concept is the reflection the individual sees of themselves in the mirror constituted by the views that others hold of the individual. As such, reflected appraisal is a corollary of the general proposition of "self reflects society": self-concept reflects others' attitudes which are a constituent part of the social schemas.

Domain of application. Reflected appraisal has been used in the literature to explain the social origins of all three aspects of self-concept: self-identification, self-evaluation, and self-emotion. However, this social mechanism is most effective "for attributes that are defined in terms of the perceptions of others" (Felson 1985: 71).[18] Examples of such attributes are the individual's beliefs about their reputation, popularity, and attractiveness in the eyes of others, for in this domain of self-concept formation the opinions of others both define and measure the given attribute of the individual. When a young girl says, "I am a good sister because I look after my little brother," the self-appraisal of the girl essentially reflects what her caregivers told her: "you are a good sister because you look after your little brother." In this instance, the social agent is the child's primary caregivers (e.g., the girl's parents) who convey to the young child three important pieces of information about the child: (1) *standards of conduct*: looking after someone else is a good behavior, (2) *measurement of the conduct*: you have looked after your little brother, and (3) *social appraisal*: you are a good child. By accepting this social appraisal of her, the child also accepts the standards for and the evaluation of her conduct.

Cooley (1956 [1902]) called this type of self-concept that results from reflected appraisal the "social self" of the individual.[19] Specifically, Cooley differentiated three elements of the social self: one's imagination of others' perceptions of the concerning attribute (e.g., looking after one's little brother), one's imagination of others' judgment of that attribute (e.g., a good sister), and the resulting feelings one has about oneself (e.g., happy and proud). One more element is implied in Cooley's formulation: one's recognition of the standards of conduct endorsed by others (e.g., looking after someone else is a good behavior). In the situation of reflected appraisal, the social agent is in a position to both define the standards of conduct and evaluate the concerning attributes of the individual, and the individual is mostly on the receiving end accepting the judgment of the social agent. However, it needs to be emphasized that the appraisal the individual receives is the attitudes of the social agent the individual perceives, and this *perceived appraisal* may not correspond to the social agent's *actual appraisal* of the individual, for the individual has no direct access to the mind of the social agent.[20] It is through the combination of observation and "imagination" that the individual imputes the attitudes of the social agent.

Significant others. The self-appraisal of the individual reflects the perceived appraisals others have of the individual, but not all others are equally influential in terms of the impact of their appraisals on the individual. Based on the way an individual is embedded in society, the individual forges differential ties with others in different domains of social life, e.g., economic, political, emotional, and spiritual. And those whose opinions the individual cares about and trusts become the significant others to the individual, and it is the attitudes of those significant others that exert important influences on the individual. The more significant the others are to the individual, the more weight their opinions carry, and the more impact their opinions have on the self-appraisal of the individual. Parents and teachers, for example, are significant others to young children and have considerable influence on the formation of the children's self-concepts. Significant others also include an individual's heroes and idols who may be dead, fictional, or imaginary. Even though they have never been in contact with the individual in real life, those significant others can act as "better possible social judges" (James 1918 [1890]: 315)[21] in the mind of the individual and their verdicts might override the opinions of the real people.

Life experience. Standards of conduct are a core component of reflected appraisal. Significant others provide not only an assessment of the individual but, more importantly, the criterion for that assessment. Internalization of the assessment criterion gives rise to the self-values that the individual adopts for self-guidance and self-evaluation. However, self-values also come from other sources, including the individual's personal life experiences in society, particularly "the consequences and products of behavior that are attributed to the self as an agent in the environment" (Gecas and Schwalbe 1983: 79).[22] The influence of significant others on the self-appraisal of the individual is increasingly mediated by the individual's self-values as the life experience of the individual grows. When one lacks life experience, one's self-evaluation relies mostly on the appraisals of significant others; however, as one's life experience accumulates, one begins to "appraise the appraisals of others" (Zhao 2019).[23] The more life experience an individual gains, the more independent judgment the individual has, and the more likely the individual will question or even reject the appraisals of others that the individual deems incongruent with the established self-values.

4.2.2   Social comparison

In social comparison, one comes to learn about the social standards of conduct and the merits of one's own attributes through observing what other people do and what happens to them in the given social environment and by comparing one's own experiences in the similar environment with those of others. As the psychologist Pettigrew (1967: 243) put it, rather than taking the attitudes of significant others, in social comparison the individual learns about the social standards by observing the behavior of others and "learn[s] about themselves by comparing themselves to others."[24] Individuals also come to know social norms and themselves by comparing the outcomes of their own actions in different social situations: "We come to know ourselves, and to evaluate ourselves, from actions and their consequences and from our accomplishments and the products of our efforts" (Gecas and Schwalbe 1983: 79).[25] Through such comparisons, the individual finds out the socially sanctioned standards of conduct and uses them to guide and evaluate their own behaviors. Social comparison, therefore, provides a different mechanism by which social schemas shape the self-concept of the individual.

Domain of application. Social compassion operates under a condition of self-concept formation that is different from the condition for reflected appraisal. In reflected appraisal, significant others define the standards of conduct and evaluate the attributes of the individual, and the attitudes of significant others get reflected in the individual's self-appraisal; in social comparison, however, the individual plays a more active role in self-evaluation. The individual lives in a social environment that endorses certain ways of doing things which benefit certain groups of people. The individual learns about the prevailing social standards from the outcomes of behavior in the environment and uses learned standards to guide and assess their own actions. In many domains of social life, standards of conduct endorsed by society manifest themselves in the ongoing social practices and the attributes being evaluated are objectively measurable. For example, a boy may admit candidly that he is not good at running because he can see that most of his friends run faster than he does. The child understands that running fast is a good attribute to have (social standards of conduct) because this athletic ability is being valued in his social environment (empirical evidence), but he knows he does not seem to have that ability (self-assessment) as he runs slower than many of his friends (objectively observable). So even if his mom (significant other) were to tell him that he is a fast runner (social appraisal), he would know that it is not true. Thus, in domains of life where the standards for evaluation are known and the attributes are objectively measurable, social comparison works more effectively than reflected appraisal does in affecting self-concept. This is the reason why the original theory of social comparison proposed by Festinger (1954)[26] had a restricted scope of application focusing mostly on such personal attributes as physical characteristics, intellectual abilities, and financial conditions.[27]

Reference groups. A key element in social comparison is the reference group which serves as the frame of reference for comparison. The reference group consists of other people who the individual believes possess certain characteristics that are suitable or relevant for comparison. Usually, though not always, these are the characteristics that the individual is in favor of. People with such attributes form "a group against which we measure our actions and provide the standards to which we aspire. How we dress, talk, feel and act in different circumstances are all informed by our reference groups" (Bauman and May 2001: 25).[28] The reference group then serves as "an organized scheme" that supplies the individual with the criterion for being a successful member of society and "the value in terms of which a person estimates his own conduct" (Shibutani 2006: 260).[29] One's reference group is, in this sense, a group of people whom one identifies oneself with and measures oneself against.

Specifically, there are two different types of reference groups. One is the reference group of individuals, and the other is the reference group of categories of individuals.[30] The *reference group of individuals* consists of people from one's immediate social environment, with whom one interacts frequently and against whom one measures oneself. One's classmates, athletic teammates, coworkers, neighbors, and friends are examples of one's reference group of individuals. These individuals are part of the world of one's everyday life and can form different subgroups of reference for comparison of different attributes of the individual (e.g., grades, athletic abilities, and financial situations). The accomplishments and failures of those in the reference group provide aspirations and lessons for the individual. By comparing oneself to others in the relevant areas, one learns about one's strengths and weaknesses which can lead to the reassessment of one's goals and plans for future actions.

Moreover, one also compares oneself to the *reference group of categories of individuals*.[31] This type of reference groups consists of social categorizations of individuals, real or imaginary, with whom one identifies as sharing certain common characteristics, such as nationality, race, class, gender, and age. These are the characteristics that society uses to lump individuals into different categories marked by stereotypical attributes, and these stereotypes carry positive or negative valences that reflect the prevailing values of society. Seeing oneself as a member of a given category of individuals, one is likely to evaluate oneself in terms of the stereotypical attributes attached to that category and to also compare oneself to the stereotypes associated with other categories of individuals for purposes of self-verification. As such, social categorizations are not only descriptive but prescriptive and evaluative as well, "serv[ing] as standards guiding the verification process" (Burke 2004: 9).[32]

Choice of reference groups. Reference groups constitute the coordinate system of the individual's lifeworld, and they help the individual find out where they are relative to the locations of others in society. What type of reference groups an individual chooses for social comparison largely depends on where the individual is situated in society. The birth of the individual into a given family, for example, determines the neighborhood in which the individual lives, the schools the individual attends, and the peers the individual interacts with. In the beginning, one compares oneself mostly to others in one's immediate social environment. For any given attribute, say, personal income, three different types of social comparison can be conducted by the individual: *upward comparison* in which one compares oneself to others who are better off than one is, *downward comparison* in which one compares oneself to others who are worse off than one is, or *lateral comparison* in which one compares oneself to others who are the same as one is.[33] Those different comparisons will produce different assessments of, and feelings about, oneself. As one's contact with, and knowledge of, the world increases through education, occupation, and other means of social engagement, one's reference groups extend to include people from outside of one's immediate social environment and the categorizations of individuals that one never knew about before. The inclusion of such people and categorizations of individuals for comparison expands one's social horizon by providing new aspirations for life and new criteria for self-evaluation.

4.2.3   Cultural conditioning

Cultural conditioning is the third mechanism by which social schemas enter into the constitution of the individual's self-concept. In reflected appraisal, social schemas shape self-concept through the attitudes of significant others toward the individual. In social comparison, social schemas affect self-concept through the reference groups that the individual uses for self-assessment. And in cultural conditioning, social schemas come to influence self-concept through the cultural artifacts that make up the symbolic world in which human individuals live. As defined by Sewell (1992: 13),[34] *cultural artifacts* are objects produced by humans that are "instantiations and embodiments of schemas, they therefore inculcate and justify the schemas as well." Being surrounded by cultural artifacts in everyday life, individuals come to adopt the values and orientations associated with the given schemas through prolonged exposure and progressive assimilation. In due time, the individual's self-concept becomes congruent with the prevailing social schemas embedded in the surrounding cultural artifacts. This gradual process of progressive cultural influence on self-concept formation is named here *cultural conditioning.*

Domain of application. Cultural conditioning is a mechanism for transmitting the tacit knowledge of the "rules of social life" (Geertz 1973)[35] to the members of society. A large part of social knowledge is tacit in nature as the rules of social life are not fully articulable; nevertheless, most members of society are knowledgeable enough to understand what the rules are and how to follow them in their daily activities. Social conventions and customs regarding language use, interpersonal greeting, turn-taking in conversations, and the display of emotions in public are all forms of tacit knowledge. Such knowledge also provides individuals with the criteria for self-regulation and self-assessment. For example, how to manage one's body, perform gender, share thoughts, and express intimate feelings? This type of knowledge pertains to the "technologies of the self" (Foucault 1988)[36] and is inherently tacit. Even though they are indispensable in social life, such behavioral codes cannot be effectively taught in classroom, only to be "tacitly grasped" (Giddens 1984: 22)[37] by individuals in social practice through the mechanism of cultural conditioning. Cultural scripts and the generalized other are two essential elements involved in cultural conditioning.

Cultural scripts. Social schemas exist in explicit or implicit forms. The explicit form of social schemas includes stipulated rules and regulations, such as laws and constitutions; and the implicit form of social schemas consists of unstipulated rules and regulations, such as customs and conventions. Implicit social schemas are cultural scripts:

> Cultural scripts are above all concerned with things that one can or cannot say, things that one can or cannot do, and also things that "it is good" to say or do. They constitute a society's unspoken "cultural grammar" (whose parts can surface, at times, in open discourse, in the form of proverbs, common sayings, popular wisdom, common socialization routines, and so on). (Wierzbicka 1994: 19)[38]

Cultural scripts, which constitute "a tacit system of cultural rules" (Wierzbicka 1994: 12),[39] contain implicit knowledge of proper ways of behaving in society. While language plays a pivotal role in the functioning of cultural scripts, messages contained in cultural scripts cannot be fully explicated in words because they often exist as subtexts in between the lines or as "expressions given off" that need to be inferred based on the expressions given (Goffman 1959).[40] Cultural scripts are also embedded in the designs of physical objects, such as architectures, interior decorations, public parks, social media platforms, or even something as simple as teacups, cereal boxes, and shopping bags, because those designs all "incorporate or actualize schemas" (Sewell 1992: 13).[41] Social institutions, organizations, and activities express cultural scripts as well, for they also manifest the logic of social practice and the canon of philosophy.

Cultural scripts affect the self-concept of the individual either directly or indirectly. There are cultural scripts that directly promulgate rules for self-conception and self-expression. Selfies trendy on Facebook, Instagram, and TikTok, for example, show the viewers what an attractive person should look like in terms of body shape, makeup, clothing, posture, and the like. Those selfies become the standards for ideal self-images and self-presentations against which viewers measure themselves. Cultural scripts that promulgate rules for other aspects of social life have indirect impact on self-concept formation. Take the design of Chinese courtyard dwelling for example. Architecture certainly expresses esthetical preferences through the arrangement of lines and shapes in the buildings, but such physical arrangement also involves spatial articulations of social relationships. In the case of traditional Chinese courtyard houses, "walls and wall-enclosed spaces created a spatial hierarchical framework" that reinforced the patrilineal social order, "by which one's identity and sense of self were established" (see Hu 2008: 364–366).[42] Cultural scripts embedded in physical artifacts that were made for various practical purposes, therefore, exert subtle influences on the self-concepts of the individuals who use or are exposed to those artifacts.

The generalized other. Cultural scripts are an implicit form of social schemas, and social schemas are socially accepted ways of doing things which reflect the views of society. But the question is, who represents society? In reflected appraisal, the significant others of the individual represent society, and their views represent the views of society. In social comparison, the reference group the individual uses for self-assessment represents society, and the standards of the group are the standards of society. In cultural conditioning, however, society is represented by an entity called "the generalized other" (Mead 1934).[43] The generalized other is not an individual, nor is it a group of individuals, but, rather, it is an abstract construct representing "the organization of standards and evaluations that the person puts together from the community" (Franks and Gecas 1992: 54).[44] In other words, the generalized other represents the entire community in which the individual lives, and the "attitude of the generalized other is the attitude of the whole community" (Mead 1934: 154).[45]

Where is the attitude of the generalized other located? It resides diffusely in all corners of society: in the attitudes of significant others, the standards of reference groups, the structures of social institutions, the messages of social media, and the designs of buildings, gardens, clothing, hairstyles, and numerous other cultural artifacts. The attitude of the generalized other, in other words, permeates the cultural scripts that can be found everywhere in society. By constantly exposing the individual to the omnipresent "cues embedded in the physical and social environment," the attitude of the generalized other conditions the formation of the self-concept of the individual (DiMaggio 1997: 267).[46] However, the acquisition of a coherent view of the community requires a high level of conceptualization capability that enables the individual to engage in "schematic organization" or generalization of discrete information (DiMaggio 1997: 267).[47] While being in contact with cultural scripts from day one, it is not until late adolescence that individuals become capable of conceptualizing the attitude of the generalized other.[48]

The attitude of the generalized other is a symbolic system that specifies "designs for living," "rules of the game of life," "ways of dealing with social situations," and "ways to think about the self and social behavior" (see Triandis 1989: 511–512).[49] Different societies have different attitudes of the generalized other, and there can be multiple attitudes of the generalized other in a society with heterogenous cultures and traditions. The two opposite and most influential attitudes of the generalized other are *individualism* and *collectivism*, with the former giving priority to individuals over collectives and the latter subordinating individuals to collectives.[50] In correspondence to these two opposing attitudes of the generalized other, there are two different types of "self-construal" or self-conception – the *independent self-construal* and the *interdependent self-construal* (Markus and Kitayama 1994).[51] While the independent self-construal emphasizes the separation of self from others, the interdependent self-construal stresses the connectedness of self to others. Buttressed by the attitude of the generalized other, the self-construal of the individual can transcend the appraisals of significant others as well as the standards of particular reference groups, enabling the individual to resist situational influences from others. As a result, "one can use the quintessentially social, but impersonal perspective given by 'fair play' as a 'generalized other' to guide their course in a competitive situation quite independent of the opinion of others – significant or not" (Franks and Gecas 1992: 54).[52]

4.2.4   Relationships among mechanisms

Reflected appraisal, social comparison, and cultural conditioning are three principal social mechanisms that shape the self-concept of the individual. The three mechanisms come into play in a particular temporal order and the concordance among them in the promulgation of social schemas influences the outcome of self-concept formation.

Sequential ordering of mechanisms. The three social mechanisms of self-concept formation are at work throughout a person's life, but they have differential impacts on self-conception at different stages of its development. The formation of self-concept in the early years of the individual's life has been divided in the literature into several stages associated with changes in the child's cognitive ability and social environment.[53] It is the interaction between the cognitive and social factors that shapes the trajectory of the development of a child's self-concept and the sequential ordering of the three mechanisms of self-concept formation.

Reflected appraisal plays a pivotal role in the formation of self-concept in the early years of an individual's life. Reflective self-awareness is the perception of oneself from the standpoints of others, which requires the ability to take the role of the other. This role-taking capability develops in three phases: preparatory stage, play stage, and game stage.[54] The *preparatory stage* is a prelinguistic period in which the child interacts with others prior to the acquisition of language. Based on nonverbal cues, e.g., facial expression, gesture, and tone, the child learns to interpret and respond to the intentions and attitudes of others.[55] In the *play stage*, the child acquires language and learns to communicate thoughts and feelings in words. Linguistic communication enables clearer and more precise expressions of mutual expectations and evaluations among the speakers. In playing the role of the other, as in playing house, the child puts themself in the position of another person and looks at things, including themself, from that person's position. The looking-glass self of the individual emerges from this role-playing process based on the mechanism of reflected appraisal.

The mechanism of social comparison becomes increasingly important in shaping self-concept formation when the immediate social environment of the child expands to include peer groups such as classmates, neighbors, and friends. Besides the opinions of significant others such as parents and teachers, the reference groups of peers in the child's lifeworld begin to serve as an alternative source of criterion for self-assessment. For example, by comparing oneself to one's peers on physical ability, school performance, and other observable aspects of one's life, one gains a new measure of oneself, which may or may not correspond to the appraisals one receives from the significant others. Social comparison, therefore, broadens the horizon of one's self-understanding.

Cultural conditioning affects self-concept formation from the first day of the individual's life, but its impact is not apparent until the individual is able to grasp the attitude of the generalized other based on the diffused cultural scripts from the expanded social environment. Before that, the individual was only capable of perceiving the views and attitudes of significant others, e.g., particular individuals and groups. The ability to reconcile and synthesize different viewpoints of multiple sources is acquired at what Mead (1934)[56] calls the *game stage*, where one learns to generalize disparate views, attitudes, and criteria from different culture scripts (e.g., significant others, reference groups, and cultural artifacts) into a coherent and general perspective. That perspective is the perspective of "the generalized other," which represents the attitude of one's community or society. The internalization of the attitude of the generalized other gives rise to a stable set of self-values and standards that serve to guide the individual's self-perception and self-conscious action. From that point on, the individual is increasingly able to think and act according to internal self-guides, rather than being mostly dictated by the expectations of significant others or the standards of the reference groups in the immediate social environment.

Concordance of social schemas. Social schemas that enter into the self-concept of the individual through the three mechanisms may not be consistent or congruent in terms of the messages (e.g., values and standards) they promulgate. The inconsistency could occur either within a mechanism or across mechanisms. *Within-mechanism inconsistency* takes place when the messages promulgated through the same mechanism of self-concept formation are discordant. For example, in reflected appraisal the behavioral standards set by mom for the child may be different from the standards set by dad, or the teachings of the teachers at school may contradict the values of parents at home. *Cross-mechanism inconsistency*, on the other hand, refers to the discordance of messages delivered through different mechanisms of self-concept formation. For instance, significant others through reflected appraisal may say one thing, the reference groups via social comparison may indicate something very different, and the generalized other by means of cultural conditioning may promote values that are incongruent with what significant others and reference groups advocate. Incongruence of promulgated messages in the social environment can cause identity instability and fragmentation,[57] but it may also make the self-concept of the individual more adaptive and resilient, leading to "increased creativity and competence in intercultural interactions" (Hong et al. 2007: 340).[58]

No society, no matter how tight a control it has over its members, can maintain a state of *absolute concordance of social schemas* in all aspects of social life at all times. However, it is possible to achieve a localized *relative concordance of social schemas* in a person's lifeworld. Within the family, for example, parents may work together to present a "united front" in setting behavioral expectations for their children, and they may also try to confine their children's social contact only to those who share their values and worldview. Residential selection and school choice are often part of the effort by parents to maintain a level of relative concordance of social schemas for their children within a larger social environment that is heterogenous in values and standards.

4.3   Social resources and self-action

The self is an entity that the individual regards as themselves, and this perceived own existence is affected by the individual's self-concept on the one hand and self-action on the other. Self-concept enables the individual to recognize and reimagine their existence, whereas self-action enables the individual to maintain and transform their existence. The sociological study of the constitution of self must therefore look into not only how social factors shape self-concept but also how they affect self-action. The previous section has examined the influence of social schemas on the self-concept of the individual, and this section focuses on the impact of social resources on the self-action of the individual.

Self-reflection and self-regulation are important neurocognitive prerequisites of the self. While self-reflection is required for the formation of self-concept, self-regulation is needed for the execution of self-action. *Self-regulation* refers to the capability of the individual to self-consciously regulate their inner states and outer behaviors. Regulation of inner states involves the exercise of control over one's impulses, feelings, and thoughts, as well as engaging in deliberations and making choices from among perceived options. Regulation of outer behaviors, on the other hand, involves the "executive function" of initiating, monitoring, and completing a planned action.[59] According to the differences in the goals of the action, two types of executive control can be distinguished: (a) *primary control* which is the effort to change the external world to satisfy the needs of the individual, and (b) *secondary control* which is the effort to change the needs of the individual to accommodate the external world.[60] In either case, the individual seeks to strike a balance between the self and the world through self-action.

4.3.1   Forms of social resources

The self-action of an individual is conditioned by the social resources available to the individual. In the realm of action, resources are anything that actors can draw upon to increase their power of achieving their goals.[61] *Social resources* are a subset of resources that are available to the actors by virtue of their embedment in a particular segment of society. There are two major types of social resources: social position and social capital. *Social position* is the actor's location in the organizational hierarchy of an institution.[62] The power of action in this case comes from the predefined roles associated with a position in the organization which provide the incumbent of the position with designated privileges and responsibilities.[63] For example, the managerial role in a company grants the incumbent of the position certain administrative prerogatives as well as access to certain resources the company owns.

Social capital, on the other hand, is the connections the actor forges with other people in the larger social networks through which the actor is able to gain access to resources that are otherwise unavailable to them.[64] An individual located in a lower position of an organization, for example, may gain access to certain desired resources through other people who occupy higher positions in the organization with whom the individual has connections. Unlike the authority and prerogatives associated with an administrative position that are grounded in the structure of an organization, the access to resources one gains through one's social capital comes from the return of one's investment in social relationships.[65]

Social resources also include one's membership in the "major categories of social stratification and differentiation," such as class, race, gender, and ethnicity (Gecas and Burke 1995: 52).[66] Those *social categorizations* carry symbolic and material power that enables the members to have "access to different kinds and amounts of resources and hence different possibilities for transformative action" (Sewell 1992: 21).[67] Within a given societal context, individuals have differential access to resources depending on the social positions they occupy in formal organizations, the social capital they cultivate in informal social networks, and the social categorizations they fall under and identify themselves with.

4.3.2   Impacts on self-action

Access to social resources conditions the self-action of the individual. Self-action is a form of self-enactment, which involves the conscious effort of the individual to actualize their self-concept within a given social environment. Social resources come to impinge on the self-action of the individual by affecting the individual's self-efficacy beliefs as well as self-action capabilities.

Impact on self-efficacy beliefs. Self-action is affected by self-concept which includes the individual's self-efficacy beliefs. *Self-efficacy beliefs* are beliefs about one's ability to "organize and execute the courses of action required to produce given attainments" (Bandura 1997: 3),[68] in other words, they are "appraisals of our ability to use our competencies in specific domains and situations ... beliefs about what we can do with our skills and abilities in certain contexts and conditions" (Maddux and Volkmann 2010: 316).[69] What one thinks one is able to accomplish is determined by one's assessment of one's own capability, relative to the perceived difficulty of the task and the conditions under which the task is to be performed. This assessment is positively related to the individual's perception of the availability of resources needed to carry out the task. Resources must be perceived by the actor as being potentially available before the actor will seek to access them, but such perceptions do not have to be correct in order to produce a positive impact on the actor's self-efficacy beliefs. If one believes that one has the necessary resources for accomplishing a desired goal, one is likely to take actions even if this belief is actually false. The overestimation of available resources will lead to an exaggeration of one's action capacity and the setting of a more ambitious goal for action. An underestimation of the resources one actually possesses, on the other hand, will result in a lower assessment of one's efficacy and less likelihood of aiming higher in one's action.

Impact on self-action capabilities. Self-action capabilities are one's ability to actualize one's self-concept through self-conscious action. Self-efficacy beliefs have an effect on self-action capacities. An inflated belief about one's self-efficacy will more likely motivate an individual to act and could make the individual persevere longer when encountering obstacles, but it can also cause an individual to underestimate the difficulties and challenges that lie ahead and thus to be less prepared for the tasks at hand. Another important factor that affects one's self-action capabilities is the social resources – social positions and social capital – that one is able to mobilize for self-actions in the areas of impression management, position management, and collaboration management. The role expectations that come with one's social positions influence the ways in which one presents oneself to others, e.g., as a supervisor, coworker, or personal friend. One's social capital, including the "weak ties" that one forged with others (Granovetter 1973),[70] is important for one's position management in the different domains of one's social life. Finally, both social position and social capital have an effect on one's collaboration management: the authority and prerogatives associated with one's social position and the connections and reputation that constitute one's social capital affect one's interactions with others.

It should be noted that while social resources are indispensable for self-action, they do not determine the purposes of their use. The same type of social resources can be used to satisfy an individual's "deep, unsocialized, inner impulses," but they can also be used by the individual to pursue communal and "institutionalized goals" (see Turner 1976: 991–992).[71] Within an institutional organization, some people use their positions and connections to maintain the status quo that benefits themselves, others act as "institutional entrepreneurs" who seek to "break with the rules and practices associated with the dominant institutional logic(s)" (Battilana 2006: 657).[72] In other words, social resources enhance the individual's capacity for self-action, but it is the individual's self-values that determine the type of self-action the individual will undertake given the available resources.

4.4   Cross effects of schemas and resources

Society shapes the constitution of the self of the individual through the influence of social schemas and social resources. Social schemas affect self-concept and social resources affect self-action; in addition, social schemas have an indirect effect on self-action and social resources have an indirect effect on self-concept. Because self-action is guided by self-concept, particularly self-values, social schemas indirectly affect self-action by shaping the self-concept of the individual. For example, if one believes that "slim is beautiful," one is likely to engage in weight loss. Therefore, the social schema that promotes the idea of "slim is beautiful" indirectly contributes to the prevalence of certain types of eating behavior. Likewise, social resources can influence the self-concept of the individual by favoring certain types of self-action. As Bandura (1995: 3)[73] remarks, successes in one's action build a robust belief in one's self-efficacy, for "[t]he most effective way of creating a strong sense of efficacy is through mastery experiences. They provide the most authentic evidence of whether one can muster whatever it takes to succeed." The distribution of social resources in a given way can therefore enhance certain self-efficacy beliefs by making a certain type of self-action more likely to succeed.

4.5   Conclusion

The self of the individual is a product of society. The embedment of the individual in society and the neurocognitive capacities for self-reflection and self-regulation are important prerequisites for the possession of the self. However, it is the structure of society that shapes the self of the individual: social schemas influence the formation of self-concept and social resources affect the execution of self-action. The self is what the individual perceives and acts toward as their own existence, but the way in which the individual does that largely depends on the characteristics of the society in which the individual is embedded. In that sense, it is indeed true that self reflects society.

However, this raises a question about the functionality of the self. Given that the self is a social product, does that product have a social function? Does society need its members to have selves? If self is impossible without society, is society possible without self? The sociological research on this topic has mostly focused on the impact of the self on the behavior of the individual at the micro level of social interaction, and more studies are needed to understand the importance of the self for the constitution and functioning of social institutions at the macro level of society. The next chapter examines the roles that the self plays in human society at both micro and macro levels.

Notes

1. Maria Legerstee (1999) 'Mental and bodily awareness in infancy: Consciousness of self-existence,' in S. Gallagher and J. Shear (eds.), *Models of the Self*. Exeter, UK: Imprint Academic, pp. 213–230.
2. There are debates in the literature over whether certain social animals such as chimpanzees have a rudimentary level of conceptual self-awareness. See Thomas Suddendorf and Andrew Whiten (2001) 'Mental evolution and development: Evidence for secondary representation in children, great apes, and other animals,' *Psychological Bulletin*, 127(5), 629–650.
3. Alain Morin (2011) 'Self-awareness part 2: Neuroanatomy and importance of inner speech,' *Social and Personality Psychology Compass*, 5(12), 1004–1017.
4. P. K. McGuire, D. A. Silbersweig, R. M. Murray, A. S. David, R. S. J. Frackowiak, and C. D. Frith (1996) 'Functional anatomy of inner speech and auditory verbal imagery,' *Psychological Medicine*, 26, 29–38.
5. Tiffany W. Chow and Jeffrey L. Cummings (1999) 'Frontal-subcortical circuits,' in B. L. Miller and J. L. Cummings (eds.), *The Human Frontal Lobes: Functions and Disorders*. New York: Guilford Press, pp. 3–26.
6. David J. Turk, Todd F. Heatherton, C. Neil Macrae, William M. Kelley, and Michael S. Gazzaniga (2003) 'Out of contact, out of mind: The distributed nature of the self,' *Annals New York Academy of Sciences*, 1001, 65–78.
7. Georg Wilhelm Friedrich Hegel (1977 [1807]) *Phenomenology of Spirit*, tr. A. V. Miller. Oxford: Oxford University Press.
8. Herbert Blumer (1969) *Symbolic Interactionism: Perspective and Method*. Berkeley: The University of California Press.

9. Eric I. Knudsen (1999) 'Early experience and critical periods,' in M. J. Zigmond (ed.), *Fundamental Neuroscience*. San Diego, CA: Academic Press, pp. 637–654.
10. William H. Sewell, Jr. (1992) 'A theory of structure: Duality, agency, and transformation,' *American Journal of Sociology*, 98(1), 1–29.
11. George H. Mead (1934) *Mind, Self, and Society: From the Standpoint of a Social Behaviorist*. Chicago: The University of Chicago Press.
12. Anthony Giddens (1984) *The Constitution of Society: Outline of the Theory of Structuration*. Berkeley: University of California Press.
13. Sheldon Stryker and Peter J. Burke (2000) 'The past, present, and future of an identity theory,' *Social Psychology Quarterly*, 63(4), 284–297.
14. Anthony Giddens (1984).
15. William H. Sewell, Jr. (1992).
16. Hazel Markus (1977) 'Self-schemata and processing information about the self,' *Journal of Personality and Social Psychology*, 35(2), 63–78.
17. Charles H. Cooley (1956 [1902]) 'Human nature and the social order,' in R. C. Angell (ed.), *The Two Major Works of Charles H. Cooley: Social Organization [and] Human Nature and the Social Order*. Glencoe, IL: Free Press, pp. 1–451.
18. Richard B. Felson (1985) 'Reflected appraisal and the development of self', *Social Psychology Quarterly*, 48(1), 71–78.
19. Charles H. Cooley (1956 [1902]).
20. For more discussions on this, see Shanyang Zhao (2014) 'Self as an emic object: A re-reading of William James on self,' *Theory & Psychology*, 24(2), 199–216.
21. William James (1950 [1890]) *The Principles of Psychology* (Vol. 2). New York: Dover.
22. Viktor Gecas and Michael L. Schwalbe (1983) 'Beyond the looking-glass self: Social structure and efficacy-based self-esteem,' *Social Psychology Quarterly*, 46, 77–88.
23. Shanyang Zhao (2019) 'Bringing self-values back in: From reflected appraisal to appraised appraisal,' in N. Ruiz-Junco and Baptiste Brossard (eds.), *Updating Charles H. Cooley: Contemporary Perspectives on a Sociological Classic*. New York: Routledge, pp. 126–140.
24. Thomas F. Pettigrew (1967) 'Social evaluation theory: Convergences and applications,' *Nebraska Symposium on Motivation*, 15, 241–311.
25. Viktor Gecas and Michael L. Schwalbe (1983).
26. Leon Festinger (1954) 'A theory of social comparison,' *Human Relations*, 7, 117–140.
27. Abraham P. Buunk and Frederick X. Gibbons (2007) 'Social comparison: The end of a theory and the emergence of a field,' *Organizational Behavior and Human Decision Processes*, 102, 3–21.
28. Zygmunt Bauman and Tim May (2001) *Thinking Sociologically*. Malden, MA: Blackwell.
29. Tamotsu Shibutani (2006) 'Reference groups as perspectives,' in J, O'Brien (ed.), *The Production of Reality*. Thousand Oaks, CA: Pine Forge Press, pp. 257–262.

30. See Peter J. Burke (2004) 'Identities and social structure: The 2003 Cooley-Mead award address,' *Social Psychology Quarterly*, 67(1), 5–15; Jan E. Stets and Peter J. Burke (2000) 'Identity theory and social identity theory,' *Social Psychology Quarterly*, 63(3), 224–237.

31. A key difference between the reference group of individuals and the reference group of categories of individuals is that one compares oneself with specific individuals in the former case and with categorizations of specific roles in the latter case. See Jan E. Stets and Peter J. Burke (2000).

32. Peter J. Burke (2004).

33. Hart Blanton, Abraham P. Buunk, Frederick X. Gibbons, and Hans Kuyper (1999) 'When better-than-others compares upward: The independent effects of comparison choice and comparative evaluation on academic performance,' *Journal of Personality and Social Psychology*, 76, 420–430; Frederick X. Gibbons, David J. Lane, Meg Gerrard, Monica Reis-Bergan, Carrie L. Lautrup, Nancy A. Pexa, and Hart Blanton (2002) 'Comparison-level preferences after performance: Is downward comparison theory still useful?' *Journal of Personality and Social Psychology*, 84, 865–880.

34. William H. Sewell, Jr. (1992).

35. Clifford Geertz (1973) *The Interpretation of Culture*. New York: Basic.

36. Michel Foucault (1988) 'Technologies of the self,' in L. H. Martin, H. Gutman, and P. H. Hutton (eds.), *Technologies of the Self: A Seminar with Michel Foucault*. Amherst, MA: University of Massachusetts Press, pp. 16–49.

37. Anthony Giddens (1984).

38. Anna Wierzbicka (1994) '"Cultural scripts": A semantic approach to cultural analysis and cross-cultural communication,' *Pragmatics and Language Learning Monograph Series*, 5, 1–24.

39. Ibid.

40. Erving Goffman (1959) *The Presentation of Self in Everyday Life*. New York: Doubleday.

41. William H. Sewell, Jr. (1992).

42. Xiao Hu (2008) 'Boundaries and openings: Spatial strategies in the Chinese dwelling,' *Journal of House and the Built Environment*, 23, 353–366.

43. George H. Mead (1934).

44. David D. Franks and Viktor Gecas (1992) 'Autonomy and conformity in Cooley's self-theory: The looking-glass self and beyond,' *Symbolic Interaction*, 15(1), 49–68.

45. George H. Mead (1934).

46. Paul DiMaggio (1997) 'Culture and cognition,' *Annual Review of Sociology*, 23, 263–287.

47. Ibid.

48. Susan Harter (1999) *The Construction of the Self: A Developmental Perspective*. New York: Guilford.

49. Harry C. Triandis (1989) 'The self and social behavior in differing cultural contexts,' *Psychological Review*, 96(3), 506–520.

50. Ibid.

51. Hazel Rose Markus and Shinobu Kitayama (1994) 'Culture and the self: Implications for cognition, emotion, and motivation,' *Psychological Review*, 98(2), 224–253.
52. David D. Franks and Viktor Gecas (1992).
53. For example, Harter divides the normal development of the self in the early years of an individual's life into three periods: early childhood, middle childhood, and late childhood, each marked with distinctive characteristics of cognitive and environmental changes. See Susan Harter (1999).
54. George H. Mead (1934). The "play stage" and "game stage" of self-concept formation are well known in the literature, but the "preparatory stage" has been less emphasized.
55. Some of those facial recognition capabilities, particularly anger recognition, appear to be genetically given. See Joseph D. LaBarbera, Carroll E. Izard, Peter Vietze, and Sharon A. Parisi (1976) 'Four- and six-month-old infants' visual responses to joy, anger, and neutral expressions,' *Child Development*, 47(2), 535–538.
56. Ibid.
57. Stefan Sveningsson and Mats Avesson (2003) 'Managing managerial identities: Organizational fragmentation, discourse and identity struggle,' *Human Relations*, 56(10), 1163–1193.
58. Ying-Yi Hong, Ching Wan, Sun No, and Chi-Yue Chiu (2007) 'Multicultural identities,' in S. Kitayama and D. Cohen (eds.), *Handbook of Cultural Psychology*. New York: Guilford, pp. 323–340.
59. Roy F. Baumeister, Brandon J. Schmeichel, and Kathleen D. Vohs (2007) 'Self-regulation and the executive function: The self as controlling agent,' in A. W. Kruglanski and E. T. Higgins (eds.), *Social Psychology: Handbook of Basic Principles*. New York: The Guilford Press, pp. 516–539.
60. Fred Rothbaum, John R. Weisz, and Samuel S. Snyder (1982). 'Changing the world and changing the self: A two process model of perceived control,' *Journal of Personality and Social Psychology*, 42, 5–37.
61. Anthony Giddens (1984).
62. Pierre Bourdieu (1990) *The Logic of Practice*, tr. R. Nice. Cambridge: Polity.
63. Julie Battilana (2006) 'Agency and institutions: The enabling role of individuals' social position,' *Organization*, 13(5), 643–676.
64. Mark S. Granovetter (1973) 'The strength of weak ties,' *American Journal of Sociology*, 78, 1360–1380.
65. Nan Lin (2000) *Social Capital*. Cambridge: Cambridge University Press.
66. Viktor Gecas and Peter W. Burke (1995) 'Self and identity,' in K. S. Cook, G. A. Fine, and J. S. House (eds.), *Sociological Perspective on Social Psychology*. Boston, MA: Allyn and Bacon, pp. 41–67.
67. William H. Sewell, Jr. (1992).
68. Albert Bandura (1997) *Self-Efficacy: The Exercise of Control*. New York: Freeman.
69. James E. Maddux and Jeffrey Volkmann (2010) 'Self-efficacy,' in R. H. Hoyle (ed.), *Handbook of Personality and Self-Regulation*. Hoboken, NJ: Wiley-Blackwell, pp. 315–331.
70. Mark S. Granovetter (1973).

71. Ralph H. Turner (1976) 'The real self: From institution to impulse,' *American Journal of Sociology*, 81(5), 989–1016.
72. Julie Battilana (2006).
73. Albert Bandura (1995) 'Exercise of personal and collective efficacy in changing societies,' in A. Bandura (ed.), *Self-Efficacy in Changing Societies*. Cambridge: Cambridge University Press, pp. 1–45.

Further reading

Burke, Peter J. (2004), 'Identities and social structure: The 2003 Cooley–Mead award address,' *Social Psychology Quarterly*, 67(1), 5–15.

Giddens, Anthony (1984), *The Constitution of Society: Outline of the Theory of Structuration*. Berkeley: University of California Press.

Sewell, William H. Jr. (1992), 'A theory of structure: Duality, agency, and transformation,' *American Journal of Sociology*, 98(1), 1–29.

Zhao, Shanyang (2019), 'Bringing self-values back in: From reflected appraisal to appraised appraisal,' in N. Ruiz-Junco and Baptiste Brossard (eds.), *Updating Charles H. Cooley: Contemporary Perspectives on a Sociological Classic*. New York: Routledge, pp. 126–140.

5 Social functions of the self

The sociological study of the self has largely focused on the social determinants of the self. The main question sociologists seek to answer has been: How do the social factors, which range from interpersonal contact and group memberships to institutional arrangements and cultural traditions, influence the constitution of the self? In those analyses, the self is treated as a *social product* shaped by social structure and patterns of human interaction. However, there has also been some sociological research that examines the *social impact* of the self, where the question to be answered is virtually reversed: How does the self affect human interaction and social structure? That is, how does the possession of a self by the individual influence the way in which humans interact with one another and the way human society is organized and functions? While agreeing with psychologists that "self-views do matter" (Swann et al. 2007: 84)[1] and what individuals think of themselves affects how they act in society, many sociologists tend to be wary of the view that self affects the society that shapes it, for this reciprocal argument would lead to the tautological trap that explains the cause in terms of its effect. For this reason, research on the social impact of the self in sociology has been mostly restricted to the study of the influence of the self on the *social behavior* of the individual, rather than on the *society* in which such behavior takes place.

Social behavior of the individual as studied by sociologists involves the activities of individuals "in various institutional realms" such as economic, political, educational, and legal institutions (Rosenberg 1981: 614).[2] Empirical research has shown that self-concept, particularly self-esteem, has an impact on the individual's academic achievement, occupational choice, political and civic participation, and marital relationship, among other things.[3] In the sense that the self-perception of the individual influences the individual's social conduct and relationship with others, it has been argued that the self is not just a social product but a *social force* as well.[4] Although sociologically important, this line of research on the social impact of the self suffers two main weaknesses. First, it equates self with self-concept, focusing mostly on self-esteem. Moreover, it looks at the impact of self-concept on the behavior of the individual in the institutional settings rather than on the institution itself in which the behavior of the individual takes place. Does the self, including both self-concept and self-action, affect the formation and functioning of social institutions? Would human society still be organized in the way it is if the members of society were not self-reflective and self-regulative? In other words, if it is true that self is impossible without society, is *human* society possible without self? These are fundamentally important sociological questions and sociologists are in fact better positioned to answer them.

This chapter examines the impact of the self on the constitution of society, focusing on the role the self plays in *human cooperative activity*. Society is a form of cooperation among conspecific individuals. Human society shares many commonalities with animal societies, but there is at least one thing that unequivocally distinguishes human society from all animal societies: *institutional regulation of interactions among individuals*. The evolutionary psychologist Tomasello (2009: xii),[5] for example, has observed that no animal societies "have anything even vaguely resembling" the structure of social institutions. The institutions of human society are created by humans through human cooperative activity in which the self of the individual plays a critical role. Specifically, there are two types of reflective self-awareness: situational and normative. *Situational self-awareness* emerges in the context of copresence where individuals interact with one another in evolving and transient situations, whereas *normative self-awareness* arises under the influence of the generalized other through linguistic communication.[6] These two types of self-awareness are needed for two different modes of human cooperative activity: situational self-awareness for situational cooperative activity and normative self-awareness for normative cooperative activity. While certain select species of animals also have situational self-awareness, only humans are known to possess normative self-awareness, a unique interactive capability that makes human institutional self-regulation possible.

5.1   Human cooperative activity

A distinctive form of human activity is *human cooperative activity*,[7] also known as *joint action*.[8] All social animals cooperate to a certain extent for survival and reproductive success as cooperation yields benefits that solitary living is unable to bring about for these organisms, but none of the members of other social species cooperate in the way human individuals do. In most animal societies, cooperation among conspecifics is based on a combination of genetically programmed instincts (e.g., division of labor in ant colonies) and imprinted habits (e.g., collective hunting in wolf packs). Only humans and a few other select species such as chimpanzees and dolphins are capable of engaging in cooperative activities based on "*shared intentionality*," i.e., "the ability to create with others joint intentions and joint commitments in cooperative endeavors" (Tomasello 2009: xiii).[9] But, unlike the members of other select species that forge their shared intentionality exclusively on the basis of situational calculations, human individuals are able to construct their shared intentionality in the form of institutional rules, which makes human cooperative activity unique.

Human collaboration is a sequence of joint activities that consists of four major steps: common attention, collaborative intention, collective planning, and action alignment. The self is needed for three of the four steps in the construction of mutual knowledge and the coordination of individual activities for the achievement of common goals.

5.1.1   Common attention

Common attention refers to the awareness of the same object by different individuals. If individuals are not paying attention to the same object, cooperation among them in regard to that object is out of the question. However, individuals may attend to the same object without knowing that others are doing the same. Common attention is formed when individuals are aware that they are all attentive toward to the same object. This notion of common attention, also known as "*joint attention*"[10] is "triadic" in nature, involving the simultaneous awareness of oneself, others, and the target object.[11] For example, a boy is interested in a toy nearby and the boy knows that a girl nearby is also interested in that toy, and the same is true for the girl. Research has found that the ability to form common attention emerges between 6 and 12 months of age in human infants and it becomes well established by 18 months of age.[12] Not coincidentally, this is also the time when the self begins to emerge in young children.[13] The possession of the self enables individuals to have *recursive awareness* of common attention, i.e., one's awareness that others are aware of one's attention to the same object. To continue with the previous example, the boy is not only aware that the girl nearby is interested in the same toy but is also aware that the girl knows he is also interested in the toy. This kind of recursive awareness is not necessary for human cooperative activity at this stage but becomes essential later on.

5.1.2 Collaborative intention

Common attention in itself does not generate collaborative intention. When individuals pay common attention to an object, they may have different intentions for what to do about that object. Some may lose interest in that object and walk away, others may keep attending to it but do nothing else, and still others may decide to go for the object and are willing to fight with others for obtaining it. None of the above is cooperative activities, of course. Two additional factors must be in place before a collaborative intention can be formed: (1) the sharing of a common goal and (2) the commitment to collaborate with others for achieving the common goal. Merely having a common goal is insufficient because individuals may aim for the same object without the intention to assist one another in obtaining the object. Commitment for collaboration occurs in certain situations the individuals encounter. One such situation is that the task the individuals face is not easily achievable by anyone acting alone (e.g., to fend off an attack by a pack of wolves) *and* the individuals believe that they will benefit from helping one another (e.g., avoid being hurt or killed by the vicious attacking wolves). Thus, collaborative intention is undergirded by a motivational factor.

There is another aspect of collaborative intention that must be noted. The fact that all individuals have collaborative intentions does not necessarily mean that all individuals *know* that they are all intent on collaborating. Individuals' intention for collaboration must be communicated to others to form a *collective intention* for cooperation, i.e., a "*we-intention*."[14] The self plays a pivotal role in the creation of such mutual knowledge. To form a "we-intention" for collaboration, individuals must be able to judge what others are up to, convey to others what their own intentions are, change others' intentions, or modify their own to forge a shared common intention. This is a process that involves perspective-taking, self-reflection, self-control, and mutual influence, a process that would be impossible without all participating individuals possessing the capacities for being self-reflective and self-regulative.

5.1.3   Collective planning

The establishment of a collaborative intention among the individuals leads to the next step in human cooperative activity: the creation of a cooperative plan. When two individuals have a shared intention for collaboration, they also need to know how to align their activities so that the joint effort can bring about the outcome they both desire. That type of mutual knowledge for what to do is called the *cooperative plan*, i.e., the specification of the different roles individuals or groups of individuals are expected to play in the collective effort to accomplish a common goal. Depending on the nature of the task at hand, the amount of planning can be minimal, allowing collaborators to improvise based on the unfolding of the situation, and it can also be elaborate, meticulously laying out all possible situational scenarios and the various collective responses that would be called for. In animal societies, there are "operating manuals" or "algorithms" for collaboration among conspecific individuals,[15] but those cooperative plans are either genetically programmed or imprinted in early life. In human cooperative activity, on the other hand, instructions for collaboration are created by humans themselves according to the situations they perceive, a challenging endeavor that requires the possession of self by all participants.

Having selves enables individuals to take the perspectives of others and to adjust their own positions in light of the expectations others hold for them. In some situations, individuals are able to improvise cooperative plans right on the spot based only on the nonverbal cues from the partners, such as gestures, facial expressions, or postures. But such plans are unavoidably simple and haphazard, hampered by unpredictable situational exigencies and the limitations of nonverbal communication. The formulation of an elaborate cooperative plan requires more time for planning and, more importantly, the use of language. Language is a system of symbols representing designated objects, which can be real or imaginary, and the objects constitute the meanings of the symbols used for communication. Language enables humans to move beyond the limits of "here and now" to communicate about the world of "there and then," things that are remote, intangible, or even nonexistent. Language use presupposes the possession of self by the user. To use a language is to exchange intersubjectivity, to share one's views with others, and to look at things from the perspectives of others. In planning for collaboration, individuals seek to anticipate the evolving situation, place themselves in that situation, and specify the things that need to be done and the roles they expect each other to play, while leaving room for necessary improvisation in response to unanticipated occurrences in the emerging situation. Obviously, if the individual has no self-awareness and is unable to take the view of the other, collective planning for cooperative activity would be out of the question; it would also be impossible to plan for cooperation beyond the immediacy of situational copresence without the use of language.

5.1.4   Action alignment

The implementation of a cooperative plan involves the alignment of individual actions to bring about the intended outcome. This action alignment is done by each individual through self-regulation according to the established plan and the continuous monitoring of the unfolding situation that may call for the change of the initial plan. In fitting one's activity to those of others, individuals "act on their expectations about others, expectations based on beliefs about others' expectations about them" (Bratman 1992: 329).[16] Such mutual expectations and responsiveness require that individuals are both self-aware and aware of others' awareness of them, and are capable of both self-regulation and the regulation of others' activities for the pursuit of a common goal. Thus, like the second and third steps in human cooperative activity, action alignment is also predicated on the possession of selves by the individuals.

In summary, human cooperative activity is a mode of interaction among individuals which consists of common attention, collaborative intention, collective planning, and the individuals' self-conscious alignment of their actions to one another in the implementation of a cooperative plan. Depending on how much collective planning is needed for collaboration, two forms of human cooperative activity can be distinguished: situational and normative, each involving a different type of self-awareness. In *situational cooperative activity*, individuals utilize their *situational selves* to coordinate collaborations among them in evolving and unpredictable environments. In *normative cooperative activity*, on the other hand, individuals rely on their *normative selves* in the construction and implementation of institutional rules that regulate their joint activities. While certain select social animals also have situational selves, only humans are known to possess normative selves which contribute to the rise of normative human cooperative activity, essential for the functioning of human society. In Mead's words (1934: 239–240):[17]

> Given the self there is then the possibility of the further development of the society on this self-conscious basis, which is so distinct from the loose organization of the herd or from the complex society of the insects. It is the self as such that makes the distinctive human society possible.

Self and society therefore have a reciprocal relationship: the self is a product of society, and human society cannot exist and function in the way it does without the type of selves that human individuals possess. To understand human society, it is thus necessary to understand the social functions of the human self. The sections that follow examine in turn the importance of the two types of human selves – situational selves and normative selves – for human cooperative activity, and they also specify the conditions under which a given type of self is needed for a given mode of human cooperation.

5.2   Self and situational cooperative activity

Human situational cooperative activity takes place in an environment in which individuals are physically copresent, sharing the proximity of "here and now" in an emerging and developing chain of events. Proximity and uncertainty are the hallmarks of this environment. Interactions among individuals in such an environment can be nonverbal, relying exclusively on body language (e.g., facial expressions and gestures) and paralinguistic expressions (e.g., tone and pitch of voice) to convey emotions, intentions, and other meanings. In situational cooperation, individuals are mutually responsive in their effort to provide support to one another. Communication and the ascertainment of collaborative intentions are crucial for cooperative activity in uncertain situations. According to the extent to which collaborative intentions are explicitly communicated among the participating individuals, activities of situational cooperation can be divided into three types in the order of increasingly shared intentionality: *embodied attunement, nonverbal reference,* and *situational cooperative activity.* The possession of selves by individuals is not a requirement for embodied attunement and nonverbal reference, but it is necessary for situational cooperative activity.

5.2.1   Embodied attunement

Embodied attunement is a mode of human interaction in which individuals attend to each other's emotional needs, sharing and reacting supportively to the "feeling-state" of others in the absence of intentional communication for collaboration (see Jonsson and Clinton 2006: 388).[18] For example, a mom looks at her infant baby with love, the baby looks back in happiness; and the mom smiles at her baby, the baby smiles back. This chain of co-oriented acts is affect-based, spontaneous and non-reflective, involving no communication of collaborative intentions. An underlying mechanism responsible for embodied attunement has been identified as the *mirror neuron system* that establishes a direct experiential connection between observer and observed by automatically simulating in the observer the perceived behavior of the observed, and this "embodied simulation" process "constitutes a fundamental basis for an automatic, unconscious, and noninferential understanding of another's actions, intentions, emotions, sensations, and perhaps even linguistic expressions" (Gallese et al. 2007: 144).[19] Underpinned by this neuronal mechanism, embodied attunement among individuals in copresence requires neither collaborative intention nor self-awareness.

5.2.2   Nonverbal reference

The next level of situational engagement is nonverbal reference which involves the communication of collaborative intention. Collaborative intention consists of the willingness to work with others for the achievement of a common goal, but a major challenge in prelinguistic cooperation lies in the communication of collaborative intentions. *Nonverbal reference* is the attempt to recruit, without language, the attention and assistance of another individual for accomplishing a task.[20] "Pay attention to this" or "help me with that" is the kind of message to be conveyed in nonverbal reference, and, typically, an outreached arm and finger are used by one individual pointing to an intended object or event to elicit the attention and assistance of another individual. Based on the kinds of intention conveyed by the gestures, two subtypes of pointing have been differentiated. In *protoimperative pointing*, one individual asks for the assistance of another individual in getting something done, e.g., a baby points to a toy while crying and stops crying when the caregiver gets the toy to the baby. In *protodeclarative pointing*, on the other hand, one individual simply wants to share attention with another individual, e.g., a baby points at a toy to the caregiver and keeps pointing until the caregiver takes a look at it.[21] However, some researchers argue that protodeclarative pointing indicates that one individual has awareness of the intentionality of another individual, which is a higher-level cognitive ability absent in protoimperative pointing.[22]

Unlike embodied attunement, which is automatic and noninferential in mutual responsiveness, nonverbal reference, particularly protodeclarative pointing, involves conscious efforts to communicate collaborative intentions, e.g., requests for help or sharing attention. The development of the ability for nonverbal reference starts with visual attention and gaze-following in children as young as 2 to 4 months of age,[23] and by 9 months old many children are able to understand the gestures of pointing to objects in close proximity.[24] This preverbal capacity for nonverbal reference clearly has a neuronal basis, but biology alone cannot fully account for the exercise and comprehension of nonverbal reference, for "outside of any shared context, pointing means nothing" (Tomasello 2009: 73).[25] At this level of intentional communication, shared life experiences with copresent situations supply meanings to the pointing gestures without the need for individuals to have selves.

5.2.3   Situational cooperative activity

However, the possession of self becomes indispensable for situational cooperative activity, which reaches the highest level of shared intentionality in copresence. Shared intentionality involves joint intention and mutual knowledge, among other things. Joint intention consists of the shared purpose of working together to achieve a common goal, and mutual knowledge is the awareness among all parties of cooperation that they have a common goal and are working together to achieve it. Such a level of shared intentionality in situational collaboration is predicated on the fulfillment of the following three requirements: full conditions of copresence, language use, and the possession of the situational self.

The *full conditions of copresence* combine recursive awareness with the presence of individuals in close proximity. Individuals must be positioned within range of each other's naked senses and they "must sense that they are close enough to be perceived in whatever they are doing, including their experiencing of others, and close enough to be perceived in this sensing of being perceived" (Goffman 1963: 17).[26] In other words, it is not just that one is able to perceive others and be perceived by others, but also that all parties are aware that they are being perceived by others, and that this awareness of being perceived is also being perceived by others. This *recursive awareness* of common attention requires that individuals in copresence have self-awareness and the awareness of others' awareness, a cognitive ability that human infants and most animals do not possess.

Nonverbal means of communication, i.e., body language and paralinguistic expressions, remain important in situational cooperative activity, but the use of syntactic language transforms human collaboration in copresence. For one thing, language makes intentional communication indexical and subtextual. *Indexicality*[27] means that expressions made in the here and now are embedded in a larger context of there and then so that the meaning of an expression cannot be fully understood without knowledge of the past to which the expression refers. An insider joke is an example of the indexical expression. *Subtextuality* means that an expression made in a given context can contain layers of meaning, e.g., the surface meaning and the embedded meaning. Goffman (1959)[28] calls the surface or literal meaning of an expression the "expression-given" and the embedded or implied meaning of an expression the "expression-given off." As Goffman notes, deceit involves the former and feigning the latter. Situational cooperative activity, with or without language use, requires that all interlocuters possess situational selves and the capacity for taking the perspectives of copresent others.

The *situational self* is the entity one reflects upon and acts toward as one's own existence from the standpoints of significant others. The situational self is needed for cooperative activity in copresence because of situational instability and the interpretative nature of situational human collaboration. Situational cooperative activity is a process in which individuals seek to align their activities to one another according to their interpretations of the intentions of others and the agreement they reached with others on the basis of such interpretations. This process requires that individuals must be conscious of the evolving situation, consider not only what they themselves want to accomplish but also what they think others intend to accomplish, and be able to modify their own intention as well as those of others to form a shared "we-intention" for collaborative action. To ascertain the intentions of others, individuals engage in a "dual process" (Blumer 1969: 1)[29] of indicating to others one's own intention *and* interpreting the indications made by others, both involving indexical and subtextual expressions in verbal communication. This dual process enables individuals to cooperate under the full conditions of copresence and align their activities to one another based on their interpretations of the situation.

A defining characteristic of situational cooperative activity is that the situation of collaboration is evolving and unpredictable, and this uncertainty renders rigid and elaborate planning for cooperative activity practically infeasible. As a result, situational cooperative activity always remains open-ended, subject to adjustment and modification by the participants whenever needed. In aligning their activities to one another, individuals self-consciously co-regulate their actions based on perceived situational changes, and this co-regulation constitutes the crucial mutual responsiveness in the pursuit of a common goal. The situational self is involved throughout this process, particularly in the monitoring of one's own activities as well as those of others, and in the understanding that the changes one makes to one's own activity may lead to changes in the activities of others. Such "mutually engaged co-regulated coupling"[30] enables individuals to fit their activities to one another for collaboration in an evolving and transient situation.

An illustration of situational cooperative activity can be found in the simple example of two individuals working together to carry a couch from downstairs to upstairs. The couch is heavy and needs two individuals to move it. Motivational issues aside, the two individuals must first convey their willingness to help each other relocate the couch, and then they must together decide on how to do it. They need to decide, for instance, who is to carry which side of the couch, how to make turns on the stairways without bumping the couch into the walls, and where to stop to catch a breath. However, no matter how hard they try, it is impossible for them to plan their every move beforehand, for they also have to think on their feet as they go. So, there they go: they lift the couch, edge toward the stairways, move upstairs cautiously, yell out loud to each other from time to time, and adjust to unexpected twists and turns along the way. Still, there is no guarantee that this joint effort will succeed, as a fall can happen, one of them may quit, or both may decide that the couch is simply too heavy or too big for them to carry. This kind of uncertainty is inherent in situational cooperative activity, hence the need for the involvement of situational selves in those situations.

Situational cooperative activity abounds in human society. From playground games among young children to the gathering of friends at a party to wilderness adventures in small groups, individuals participate in cooperative activities of various kinds in different situations of everyday life. The possession of situational selves by the individuals is a prerequisite of such activities. However, in modern societies people spend increasingly more time in their daily lives engaging in normative cooperative activity for which the possession of the normative self becomes necessary.

5.3   Self and normative cooperative activity

Normative cooperative activity is a mode of human collaboration that takes place in a structured social environment created and maintained by humans themselves. This structured social environment of human cooperation is called an *"institution"*, which consists of rules of behavior that regulate human interaction in different spheres of social life such as family, economy, politics, and education. Institutional rules provide stability and predictability in human collaboration that is absent in human situational cooperative activity. It is believed that in the entire animal kingdom only humans are capable of engaging in normative cooperative activity, which is regulated by and reproduces institutional rules. Two species-unique characteristics that humans possess are essential for the creation of institutions and the regulation of normative cooperative activity by the institutions: (1) syntactic language and (2) the normative self. *Syntactic language* allows humans to articulate the goals of collaboration, the rules to be followed in action, the roles to be performed by the individuals, and the consequences of failing to abide by the regulations and meet the specified expectations. The *normative self* is the entity that one reflects upon and acts toward as one's own existence from the standpoint of the community as a whole, i.e., the attitude of the generalized other, as opposed to the views of the significant others or the specific individuals in copresence that shape the situational self. Only when individuals begin to regulate their behavior according to the standards of the community does normative cooperative activity come into existence. The remainder of this section examines the importance of the normative self for the construction, function, and transformation of social institutions in which normative cooperative activity takes place.

5.3.1 Institutional construction

Institutions are the products of human design, and they are "rules of behavior that have the effect of creating sociopolitical structures serving collective functions" (Richerson and Boyd 2001: 202).[31] Institutional rules specify the roles to be played by individuals and those roles perform important functions for the operation of society. However, institutionalized roles are not tied to any particular incumbents but to the specific functions they are designed to perform. For example, an educational institution consists of the roles of school administrators and staff, the roles of teachers and students, the roles of alumni, and so on. A set of behavioral expectations, including responsibilities and privileges, are specified and the specifications are then attached to each role to be followed by any occupant of that role. Such institutional designs are guided by a "bird's-eye view" that lays out "the joint goal and complementary roles all in a single representational format" and "human collaborative activities are performed through generalized roles potentially filled by anyone, including the self" (Tomasello 2009: 68).[32] This self is not the situational self, but the normative self of the individual, which is less subject to the influence of the significant others in particular situations.

Another distinctive feature of institutional rules is the adherence of role incumbents to the role specifications based on an "agreement" established among the role players through persuasion, coercion, or other means of collective sanctions. By taking on a role in an institution, the individual is assumed to have known the behavioral expectations associated with the role and the consequences of failing to meet the specified expectations. The philosopher Searle (2015: 7) describes the construction of institutional rules as a process of "the assignment of status function" on the basis of such agreements, that have the form of "*X counts as Y*, or, more typically, *X counts as Y in context C*," and he observes that:

> Human beings have a capacity which, as far as I can tell, is not possessed by any other animal species, to assign functions to objects where the objects cannot perform the function in virtue of their physical structure alone, but only in virtue of the collective assignment or acceptance of the object or person as having a certain *status* and with that status a function. (Searle 2015: 7–8)[33]

Animals engage in sex, but not marriage; teach their young in the wild, but not in school; and have alpha males, but not government. Marriage, school, and government are institutional arrangements made by human individuals who are able to regulate their behaviors according to the "attitudes of the generalized other" which they construct.

5.3.2 Institutional functioning

The possession of the normative self by the individual is a prerequisite not only for the construction but also the routine functioning of an institution. To perform roles in a social institution, individuals must be able to exercise control over their action according to the requirements associated with the roles they agree to play, and to self-monitor and self-adjust their action to ensure that the role requirements are being fulfilled. This process also involves the monitoring of, and response to, the activities of other role occupants related to the role one performs. The exercise of such self-control and self-monitoring is based not on the expectations of any particular individual but rather on the instructions provided by the "generalized other" for the role one plays. It is to this attitude of the generalized other that the individual responds in normative cooperative activity.

Aligning action and altercasting are examples of how the normative self directs the cooperative activity of the individual in maintaining the functions of social institutions. Institutional settings are characterized by established norms and role specifications that define the situation of interaction. In those settings, individuals monitor the actions of others as well as their own to make sure that norms and rules are being observed. When violations occur, individuals take actions to correct them. *Aligning action* is the effort made by the perpetrator to mitigate the damaging effect of the untoward behavior by offering excuses, accounts, and apologies to the perpetrated, whereas *altercasting* is the effort made by the perpetrated to bring the perpetrator in line with the established norms by threatening to tarnish the perpetrator's reputation and self-image.[34] An interesting variant of aligning action is the "cooperative accounts" which are sympathetic explanations for untoward behavior offered to the offenders "in order to help them save face or repair social relationships" (Poulson et al. 2018: 145).[35] But, as Hewitt (2007: 156) points out, aligning action and altercasting are in fact two sides of the same coin, both attempting to "create an 'alignment' between the substance of social interaction, the selves of those involved, and the culture they share."[36] The communal norms or the attitudes of the generalized other are what individuals seek to conform in aligning action and altercasting.

Human cooperative activities taking place in institutional settings are normative in nature because they conform to the established norms of the institution through the efforts of the individuals guided by their normative selves. Normative selves enable individuals to fit their lines of action to one another according to the shared understanding of what they are expected to perform and how they are supposed to act as members of a community. This shared understanding is essential for the institutional regulation of social life:

> [T]he complex cooperative processes and activities and institutional func-
> tionings of organized human society are also possible only in so far as every
> individual involved in them or belonging to that society can take the general
> attitudes of all other such individuals ... and can direct his own behavior
> accordingly. (Mead 1934: 155)[37]

By taking the attitudes of the generalized other, individuals in normative cooperative activity are able to work together to maintain a stable and predictable rule system that transcends the limitations of situational variations and exigencies.

5.3.3 Institutional transformation

However, no human society is monolithic in the composition of its membership and in the attitudes of its members. Individuals located in different segments of society have different stakes and interests in life, and, hence, different perspectives and worldviews. In contemporary societies, it is often the case that individuals are under the influence of a set of divergent communal values because there is more than one generalized other in a society. The existing institutional arrangements in society are the outcome of the struggles among the different attitudes of multiple generalized others, representing primarily the attitudes of the dominant social segment.

The change of an institutional order is, therefore, the change of the attitudes of the dominant generalized other. Regardless of its causes, institutional transformations are always led by the transformation of the normative selves of the individuals who are inspired by the attitudes of a new generalized other. These individuals are "institutional entrepreneurs" (DiMaggio 1988: 14)[38] with access to organizational resources who see in the alternative institutions "an opportunity to realize interests that they value highly." The process of transforming an existing institutional order and replacing it with a new one involves a combination of situational and normative cooperative activities.

In any institutionalized society, there is always an element of situational calculation in normative cooperative activity and a certain degree of institutional influence in situational cooperative activity. The impact of the situational self becomes more salient in times of institutional change when the old institutional order is not completely collapsed, and the new order has not yet been fully established. In this transitional period, the situational selves of the "institutional entrepreneurs" play a crucial part in the selection of options from among alternative courses of action. But, even at such unique historical junctures, the influence of the normative selves remains strong, for institutional transformations call for grand narratives that inspire and unite individual members in the collective pursuit of a common cause, and the normative selves of the leaders can help identify and promote the new attitudes of the rising generalized other.

5.4 The we-mode in cooperative activity

All human cooperative activities – situational or normative – are carried out by individuals in what Tuomela (2007) has called the "we-mode."[39] In situational cooperative activity, "we" consists of individuals sharing the collaborative intention to achieve a common goal in a transient and evolving situation; in normative cooperative activity, on the other hand, "we" consists of individuals who perform assigned institutional roles based on agreed-upon arrangements. In both instances, however, "we" is not a simple summation of all the members of the collectivity, but rather the identification of the collectivity by the members themselves as a group that they belong to. There is not a "we" out there by itself detached from the first-person singular perspective of the "I," for it is through the process of "selfization" that a group of people are identified by individuals in the group as "us" as opposed to "them" and, consequently, in self-referential terms, the singular "I" becomes a part of the plural "we." "We" is, therefore, a collectivity of which "I" identifies as a member and with which "I" collaborates in the pursuit of a common goal.

When the individual acts in the we-mode as a member of a collectivity, the "I" takes into consideration the objectives and expectations of the group. Similar to the "I-mode," the "we-mode" involves a process of "self-indication in which it makes an object of what it notes, gives it a meaning, and uses the meaning as the basis for directing its action" (Blumer 1969: 14).[40] This process individualizes "we" from the standpoint of the "I." The "I" is the individual in a self-referential mode, undergirded by the species-unique neurocognitive capacities for self-reflection and self-regulation as well as the distinctive life experiences of the individual. While sharing the same neurocognitive capacities, individuals have different standpoints of the "I" due primarily to the differences in their embeddedness in society. The unique social embeddedness provides each individual with a distinctive first-personal perspective, which is shaped not just by the attitudes of others but also by the particular biography of the individual. As such, the differences in the standpoints of the "I's" are reflections of the differences in the lives of the individuals, but the extent to which these "I" standpoints differ among particular individuals is an empirical matter, ultimately determined by the level of homogeneity of the society in which the lives of these individuals are embedded.

In the sense that "we" is the selfization of a collectivity by each member, there are as many "we's" as there are different individuals in the collectivity.[41] However, none of the "we's" is exactly the same. The we-mode that each individual adopts in cooperative activity is characterized by a "dual-level intentional structure – shared focus of attention at the higher level, differentiated into perspectives at a lower level" (Tomasello 2009: 70).[42] The shared attentional focus represents the common goal of the "we" that individuals have selfized for collaboration, and the differentiated perspectives at the lower level represent the different standpoints of the "I's" from which individuals in different roles work together to achieve the common goal. The different perspectives of the "I's" also reflect the different motivations that individuals have for joining the cooperative activity. Individuals in collaboration often bring different self-interests with them, and they may mesh their personal "subplans" for participation in the cooperative activity only to a certain extent, beyond which they start to compete against one another.[43] In a way, it can be argued that competition is inherent in human cooperation, and, for that reason, human cooperative activity might be better conceptualized as collaboration among competing individuals.

The tension between collaboration and competition in human cooperative activity is often turned into a tension between "us" and "me" in the
self-identification of the individual. From the first-personal standpoint
of the "I," "me" is a part of the collectivity the individual identifies as
"us" which includes other members of the group. In the situational cooperative activity, "us" is comprised of the individual and the significant
others in copresence, and there can be as many "us's" in the eyes of the
individual as there are different situations in which significant others
reside.[44] The multiple *situational us's* identified by the individual could
be discordant with one another because the attitudes of the significant
others in different situations might not be congruent. In the normative
cooperative activity, "us" is comprised of the generalized other that represents the attitudes of the community to which the individual feels that
they belong. This *normative us* provides a coherent general framework
within which various situational us's of the individual are integrated. It is
possible, however, for an individual to have more than one normative us
because the individual may have grown up or lived in different societies.
If the norms of the different societies are incongruent, the individual may
have difficulty resolving the internal value conflicts caused by the incongruent societal norms, thereby experiencing identity disconnect, split, or
even crisis.[45]

In addition to the situational and normative us's, there is a separate "*me*"
in the self-identification of the individual. The "me" is the part of the self
that the individual regards as connected to but distinct from the "us's."[46]
The relationship between "me" and "us" is complicated. In some cases,
"me" is part of the self the individual regards as being inconsistent with or
suppressed by "us," namely, the views of the significant others and/or the
generalized other;[47] in other cases, "me" is part of the self that the individual can feel but cannot precisely articulate. Moreover, sometimes "me"
remains marginal to the identity of the individual, but other times it takes
center stage in the individual's self-identification in opposition to "us" as
the "real me," the "ideal me," or the "ultimate me" of the individual.[48] If
"us" is the internalized view of the society, where does "me" come from?
It cannot be fully anchored in the views of significant others or the norms
of institutions because that would make "me" indiscriminable from situational or normative "us's"; it cannot be fully rooted in the corporeality
of the individual either because even impulsive feelings are culturally
mediated in society.[49] As with the origins of the unique perspective of the
"I," the "me" of the individual is biographically grounded, arising out of

the intersections of the individual's biological embodiment, social embedment, and personal life experiences.[50]

Given that individuals' biographical experiences are not identical in society, the social origin[s] of selves "does not preclude wide individual differences and variations among them" (Mead 1934: 201).[51] No two selves are alike. In fact, the differences in the selves of the individuals become a primary source of innovation for situational collaboration and institutional construction. In the sociological literature, the one-sided "self reflects society" proposition has been criticized as being "socially over-determined" (Denzin 1988: 68),[52] "over-socialized" (Erickson 1995: 132),[53] or relying too much on "the opinions of others" (Gecas and Schwalbe 1983: 78).[54] Unable to account for the "novel elements" in the self-identifications of individuals, the simplified versions of the "looking-glass self" argument have been seen as "circular" (Gillespie 2005: 24).[55] Recognition of the diversity of the first-personal perspectives in human cooperative activity and the grounding of the "me" in the unique biographical experiences of the individual provide a possible solution to the tautological conundrum in explaining the relationship between self and society.[56]

The selves of individuals, while being shaped by society, are an integral part of society and can act to affect society. The impact of the self on society manifests itself not only in the social behavior of individuals within various institutional settings but, more importantly, also in the constitution, functioning, and transformation of the social institutions. Figure 5.1 illustrates the institutional engagement of self-conscious individuals in influencing the construction of social schemas and the distribution of social resources. Social schemas and social resources, which are central components of social structure, do not exist and operate by themselves; rather, it is through the cooperative activity of self-reflective and self-regulative individuals that the institutional reality of society is created, maintained, and transformed. In the sense that human society is impossible without its members possessing selves, it can be said that "no reflexivity, no society" (Archer 2007: 27).[57]

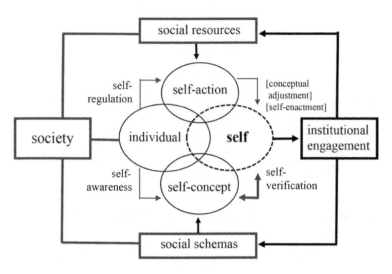

Figure 5.1   Societal functions of the self

5.5   Conclusion

This chapter has made the argument that just as self is impossible without society, society is impossible without self. However, this argument needs to be qualified to avoid fallacies. First, the relationship between self and society is not causally symmetric. To say that society affects self is to acknowledge the fact that the way individuals perceive and act toward their own existence is shaped by the structural characteristics of the society in which the individuals' lives are embedded. To say that self affects society, on the other hand, is to recognize the fact that society cannot function in the way it does if its members do not possess selves because the capacities of individuals for self-reflection and self-regulation are necessary for the institutional regulation of human cooperative activity. The word "affect" has different causal meanings in these two instances. As such, while "society *shapes* self" makes sense, "self *shapes* society" does not, for society is the environment in which self emerges, whereas self is but a necessary condition for the constitution of society.

Second, not all societies require selves. In fact, most animal societies function well without their members being self-conscious. Only a few select species in the animal kingdom have self-awareness, and only the members of human species are capable of possessing normative self-awareness. To be more precise, *Homo sapiens* have existed for about 300,000 years, but only in the last 70,000 to 50,000 years did humans acquire language and, subsequently, come to possess normative selves.[58] And it was not until after the Neolithic Revolution about 12,000 years ago that humans entered the phase of "self-selection" in human societal evolution (Zhao 2021).[59]

These qualifications bring up a new question regarding the social functions of the self: most social species in the animal kingdom live in societies without selves and a few select social species live in societies with only situational selves; how do such societies operate? Or how do members in these societies engage in cooperation? The next chapter addresses this question to further enhance the understanding of the roles that self plays in society.

Notes

1. William B. Swann, Jr., Christine Chang-Schneider, and Katie Larsen McClarty (2007) 'Do people's self-views matter? Self-concept and self-esteem in everyday life,' *American Psychologist*, 62(2), 84–94.
2. Morris Rosenberg (1981) 'The self-concept: Social product and social force,' in M. Rosenberg and R. H. Turner (eds.), *Social Psychological Perspectives*. New York: Basic Books, pp. 592–624.
3. Morris Rosenberg, Carmi Schooler, Carrie Schoenbach, and Florence Rosenberg (1995) 'Global self-esteem and specific self-esteem: Different concepts, different outcomes,' *American Sociological Review*, 60(1), 141–156; Catherine E. Ross and Beckett A. Broh (2000) 'The roles of self-esteem and the sense of personal control in the academic achievement process,' *Sociology of Education*, 73(4), 270–284; Katariina Salmela and Erik Nurmi (2007) 'Self-esteem during university studies predicts career characteristics 10 years later,' *Journal of Vocational Behavior*, 70(3), 463–477.
4. Morris Rosenberg (1981).
5. Michael Tomasello (2009) *Why We Cooperate*. Cambridge, MA: The MIT Press.
6. For more discussions on these two types of self-awareness, see Shanyang Zhao (2018) 'What is reflective self-awareness for? Role expectation for situational collaboration in alliance animal society,' *Philosophical Psychology*, 31(2), 187–209.
7. The concept of "human cooperative activity" was initially introduced by Mead. See George H. Mead (1934) *Mind, Self, and Society: From the Standpoint of A Social Behaviorist*. Chicago: The University of Chicago Press.

8. Herbert Blumer (1969) *Symbolic Interactionism: Perspective and Method.* Berkeley: University of California Press.
9. Michael Tomasello (2009).
10. Jerome S. Bruner (1975) 'From communication to language: A psychological perspective,' *Cognition*, 3, 255–287.
11. Anika Fiebich and Shaun Gallagher (2013) 'Joint attention in joint action,' *Philosophical Psychology*, 26(4), 571–587.
12. George Butterworth and Nicholas Jarrett (1991) 'What minds have in common is space: Spatial mechanisms serving joint visual attention in infancy,' *British Journal of Developmental Psychology*, 9, 55–72; Susan R. Leekam, Emma Hunnisett, and Chris Moore (1998) 'Targets and cues: Gaze following in children with autism,' *Journal of Child Psychiatry*, 39, 951–962.
13. On average, children become self-aware and able to recognize themselves in the mirror at the age of 18 months. For more discussions on the development of self in children, see Susan Harter (1999) *The Construction of the Self: A Developmental Perspective.* New York: Guilford.
14. John R. Searle (1990) 'Collective intentions and actions,' in P. Cohen, J. Morgan, and M. Pollack (eds.), *Intentions in Communication.* Cambridge, MA: The MIT Press, pp. 401–415.
15. Bert Holldobler and E. O. Wilson (2009) *The Superorganism: The Beauty, Elegance, and Strangeness of Insect Societies.* New York: W. W. Norton.
16. Michael E. Bratman (1992) 'Shared cooperative activity,' *The Philosophical Review*, 101(2), 327–341.
17. George H. Mead (1934).
18. Carl-Otto Jonsson and David Clinton (2006) 'What do mothers attune to during interactions with their infants?,' *Infant and Child Development*, 15, 387–402.
19. Vittorio Gallese, Morris N. Eagle, and Paolo Migone (2007) 'Intentional attunement: Mirror neurons and the neural underpinnings of interpersonal relations,' *Journal of the American Psychoanalytic Association*, 55(1), 131–175.
20. David A. Leavens and William D. Hopkins (1999) 'The whole hand point: The structure and function of pointing from a comparative perspective,' *Journal of Comparative Psychology*, 113, 417–425.
21. David A. Leavens, Jamie L. Russell, and William D. Hopkins (2005) 'Intentionality as measured in the persistence and elaboration of communication by chimpanzees (*Pan troglodytes*),' *Child Development*, 76, 291–306.
22. Simon Baron-Cohen (1999) 'The evolution of a theory of mind,' in M. C. Corballis and S. E. G. Lea (eds.), *The Descent of Mind: Psychological Perspectives on Hominid Evolution.* Oxford: Oxford University Press, pp. 261–277.
23. Jerome S. Bruner (1977) 'Early social interaction and language acquisition,' in H. R. Schaffer (ed.), *Studies in Mother–Infant Interaction.* New York: Academic Press, pp. 271–289.
24. H. Rudolph Schaffer (1984) *The Child's Entry into a Social World.* New York: Academic Press.
25. Michael Tomasello (2009).

26. Erving Goffman (1963) *Behavior in Public Places: Notes on the Social Organization of Gatherings*. New York: Free Press.
27. Harold Garfinkel (1967) *Studies in Ethnomethodology*. Englewood Cliffs, NJ: Prentice Hall.
28. Erving Goffman (1959) *The Presentation of Self in Everyday Life*. New York: Doubleday.
29. Herbert Blumer (1969).
30. Anika Fiebich and Shaun Gallagher (2013).
31. Peter J. Richerson and Robert Boyd (2001) 'Institutional evolution in the Holocene: The rise of complex societies,' *Proceedings of the British Academy*, 110, 197–234.
32. Michael Tomasello (2009).
33. John R. Searle (2015) 'What is an institution?' *Journal of Institutional Economics*, 1, 1–22.
34. John P. Hewitt (2007) *Self and Society: A Symbolic Interactionist Social Psychology*. Boston, MA: Pearson.
35. Stephen C. Poulson, Timothy J. Carter, and Daniel M. Crowley (2018) 'Cooperative accounts: Avoiding conflict and repairing social relations,' *Symbolic Interaction*, 41(2), 143–164.
36. John P. Hewitt (2007).
37. George H. Mead (1934).
38. Paul DiMaggio (1988) 'Interest and agency in institutional theory,' in L. Zucker (ed.), *Institutional Patterns and Organizations*. Cambridge, MA: Ballinger, pp. 3–22.
39. Raimo Tuomela (2007) *The Philosophy of Sociality: The Shared Point of View*. Oxford: Oxford University Press.
40. Herbert Blumer (1969).
41. Honneth argues that there is an "I in we," and this argument implies that there are multiple "we's" in self-identification, each corresponding to an "I." See Axel Honneth (2014) *The I in We: Studies in the Theory of Recognition*. Cambridge: Polity.
42. Michael Tomasello (2009).
43. Bratman argues that a joint activity can be cooperative down to a certain level, beyond which it can become competitive because participants may not intend to mesh their subplans all the way down. See Michael E. Bratman (1992).
44. William James said that a person "has as many different social selves as there are distinct groups of persons about whose opinion he cares." "Social selves" is the equivalent of the situational selves. William James (1918 [1890]) *The Principles of Psychology. Vol. 1.* New York: Dover, p. 294.
45. See Erik H. Erikson (1959) 'The problem of ego-identity,' *Psychological Issues*, 1, 101–164; Susan Harter, Donna B. Marold, Nancy R. Whitesell, and Gabrielle Cobbs (1996) 'A model of the effects of perceived parent and peer support on adolescent false self behavior,' *Child Development*, 67(2), 360–374.
46. Mead sometimes equated "me" with "us" which represents the internalized values of society. See George H. Mead (1934).

47. Carl R. Rogers (1951) *Client-Centered Therapy: Its Current Practice, Implications, and Theory*. Boston, MA: Houghton Mifflin.
48. This third me was called the "ultimate me" by William James (1918 [1890]); the "I-me" by George H. Mead (1934); and the "ideal self" by E. Tory Higgins (1987) in 'Self-discovery: A theory relating self and affect,' *Psychological Review*, 94(3), 319–340.
49. See discussions in Ralph H. Turner (1976) 'The real self: From institution to impulse,' *American Journal of Sociology*, 81(5), 989–1016.
50. John P. Hewitt (2007).
51. George H. Mead (1934).
52. Norman K. Denzin (1988) 'Act, language, and self in symbolic interactionist thought,' *Studies in Symbolic Interaction*, 9, 51–80.
53. Rebecca J. Erickson (1995) 'The importance of authenticity for self and society,' *Symbolic Interaction*, 18(2), 121–144.
54. Viktor Gecas and Michael L. Schwalbe (1983) 'Beyond the looking-glass self: Social structure and efficacy-based self-esteem,' *Social Psychology Quarterly*, 46(2), 77–88.
55. Alex Gillespie (2005) 'G. H. Mead: Theorist of the social act,' *Journal for the Theory of Social Behavior*, 35, 19–39.
56. Shanyang Zhao (2019) 'Bringing self-values back in: From reflected appraisal to appraised appraisal,' in N. Ruiz-Junco and B. Brossard (eds.), *Updating Charles H. Cooley: Contemporary Perspectives on a Sociological Classic*. New York: Routledge, pp. 126–140.
57. Margaret S. Archer (2007) *Making Our Way through the World: Human Reflectivity and Social Mobility*. Cambridge: Cambridge University Press.
58. Jared Diamond (2017 [1997]) *Guns, Germs, and Steel: The Fates of Human Societies*. New York: Norton.
59. Shanyang Zhao (2021) 'Human self-selection as a mechanism of human societal evolution: A critique of the cultural selection argument,' *European Journal of Social Theory*. https://doi.org/10.1177/13684310211049747

Further reading

Bauman, Zygmunt and Tim May (2001) *Thinking Sociologically*. Malden, MA: Blackwell.
Rosenberg, Morris (1981) 'The self-concept: Social product and social force,' in M. Rosenberg and R. H. Turner (eds.), *Social Psychological Perspectives*. New York: Basic Books, pp. 592–624.
Tomasello, Michael (2009) *Why We Cooperate*. Cambridge, MA: The MIT Press.
Zhao, Shanyang (2021) 'Human self-selection as a mechanism of human societal evolution: A critique of the cultural selection argument,' *European Journal of Social Theory*. https://doi.org/10.1177/13684310211049747

6   Self and animal societies[1]

In the preceding chapter it has been argued that the possession of a self by the individual is a necessary condition for the construction, functioning, and transformation of human society, but this argument must be reconciled with the fact that members of most animal societies do not have selves and those societies have been functioning well for millions of years. This apparent contradiction raises at least three questions about the relationship between self and animal society: (1) How is society possible without self for most social species in the animal kingdom? (2) Why is the possession of a self by the individual necessary in some animal societies? And (3) in what ways are human selves different from animal selves? The examination of these issues can shed further light on the constitution of society in general and the social functions of the self in particular.

The understanding of cross-species differences in societal functioning calls for the application of the perspective of natural selection. Both self and society are adaptational responses made by certain organisms to their environments for survival and reproductive success in the evolution of the species.[2] For animals living in certain environments, collaborating with conspecifics gives them survival advantages that solitary living fails to provide; and for social animals under certain selection pressures the possession of a self makes them more likely to survive and reproduce than those without the self. In examining the social functions of the self, it is therefore important to link the possession of the self to the advantages it confers on the possessors living in certain types of societies. The heuristic model of the "*Stimulus Identification and Response System*"[3] or SIRS, to be introduced in the section below, offers a useful conceptual framework for such analyses.

6.1 Identification, algorithm, and response

All biological organisms are born with a set of innate drives and needs that must be satisfied for them to survive and reproduce. The basic drives and needs include the drive for food and sex and the need for shelter and protection from predation. The necessity to fulfill those innate drives and needs in the given environment constitutes the *selection pressure* of natural evolution that compels individual organisms of a species to interact with their environment. Each organism is endowed with a stimulus identification and response system for such interaction. There are three modules in the SIRS: identification, algorithm, and response. The *identification module* consists of the organism's sensory apparatus for detecting and identifying the stimuli from the environment; the *algorithm module* is the organism's response repertory that provides the rules and instructions for reacting to the identified stimuli; and the *response module* is the organism's behavioral apparatus that enables the organism to respond to the identified stimuli based on the instructions from the algorithm module. This system is a product of the evolution of species, and it helps individual organisms interact with their environments for survival and reproductive fitness.

Modes of social response. Society is a form of adaptational response to the selection pressures individual organisms encounter in their given environment. In biology, society is commonly defined as "a cooperating group of conspecific organisms" (Wilson 2000 [1975]: 8).[4] There is wide variation in conspecific cooperation in the animal kingdom ranging from solitary but courtship and mating to division of labor in foraging and territorial defense to cohabitation of multiple generations for the communal care of young. Depending on the way in which conspecific organisms rely on one another for survival and reproductive fitness, three types of animal societies can be distinguished: *caste society, individualized society*, and *alliance society.*[5] Each society represents a distinct mode of social response adopted by the individual organisms of the given species in responding to the selection pressures they encounter in their given environment, and each mode of social response is associated with a different module of response algorithm as well as a unique submodule of social recognition.

Submodules of social recognition. A submodule of social recognition branches out from the stimulus identification module to assist social organisms in identifying the social stimuli they encounter, e.g., friendly versus hostile conspecifics. There are three levels of social recognition in the ascending order of complexity – group, individual, and self – each corresponding to a distinct type of society: *group recognition* is associated with caste society, *individual recognition* with individualized society, and *self-recognition* with alliance society. The higher level of social recognition subsumes the lower level, in other words, organisms with individual recognition are capable of group recognition, and organisms with self-recognition are capable of both group and individual recognition.

Modules of response algorithm. Upon identification of the encountered stimuli, the response algorithm module instructs the individual organism on how to respond, e.g., collaborate, fight, or retreat. Where do such response algorithms come from? They are formed differently in different types of societies: response algorithms are *genetically programmed* in caste society, *associatively learned* in individualized society, and *situationally calculated* in alliance society. These three modules of response algorithms are also hierarchically related: the associatively learned module subsumes the genetically programmed module, and the situationally calculated module subsumes the other two modules. The self is involved in the situational determination of cooperative responses, but it is absent in the selection of social responses based on genetical programs or associative learning.

Using this conceptual framework, the next three sections of the chapter examine the conditions under which the self is *not* needed for the functioning of caste and individualized animal societies, and the conditions under which the self is needed in the case of an alliance animal society. The argument to be made is that whether or not the self is required for the operation of a society depends on whether or not genetically programmed rules or associatively learned habits are sufficient for social identification and the formulation of social responses in the given environment. The possession of a self by the individual becomes necessary only when cooperation among conspecifics is based on mutual expectations developed in evolving and unpredictable situations.

6.2   Caste society and group recognition

A caste animal society is typically composed of large numbers of short-lived conspecific individuals that are segregated into stable groups or "castes" responsible for specific tasks or labor. A caste society exhibits the three principal traits of "eusociality"[6] which include (1) communal care of young, (2) division of reproductive labor, and (3) cohabitation of multiple generations. A paradigm example of the caste society is the ant colony.

Group collaboration. Ants can be found virtually anywhere on earth because they are able to survive and reproduce under enormously diverse conditions ranging from deserts to swamps. The success of ants has been attributed to their complex social organizations that facilitate communal collaboration. An ant colony is generally divided into three stable groups or "castes," each carrying out specific tasks: the queen for reproduction, the soldiers for territorial defense, and the workers that are subdivided into queen attendants, nurses, foragers, and others. Members of different castes cooperate in an orderly fashion to maintain the colony and care for the young.

Division of labor among caste members can be permanent based on mor-phological characteristics, but it can also change according to life cycle differences. In the honeybee colony, for example, each worker bee enters four distinct task groups sequentially as it ages: cleaner, nurse, food storer, and forager.[7] Either permanent or sequential, variations in caste assign-ment and labor specialization can be traced to the "underlying genetic variability" (Seeley 1995: 31)[8] of individual organisms.

Group recognition. The complex organization of an ant colony relies on an elaborate system of communication among the members, and a crucial part of that communication is group recognition, a form of social identi-fication. As Holldobler and Wilson (2009: 275)[9] have observed, "A pro-foundly important form of communication in all social insects is simply recognition – of alien species, of members of colonies of the same species, and of nestmates belonging to various castes and immature stages." Social identification in a caste society stays mostly at the *group level*, that is, the social identification module only distinguishes groups of individuals but not individuals within a group.[10] This group orientation in social identification reflects the fact that activities in caste animal society are organized based on group rather than individual characteristics.

In ant colonies, group recognition is accomplished mostly through chemical means. Each ant carries a waxy coating over its body cuticle containing a definite set of hydrocarbons. This coating is a mixture of chemical elements from several sources: those produced by the ant's own internal metabolism, those produced by other ants' internal metabolisms including the queen's, and those produced by other objects in the colony's environment. The blending of these chemical elements through mutual grooming and other means of exposure creates distinctive classes of hydrocarbons that are unique to a colony, a caste within a colony, and a group within a caste. Identification of colonial memberships and sub-groups is made by an ant using its antennae to scan the hydrocarbons in the outer layer of another ant's body cuticle. This social identification procedure is genetically determined and passed on to the younger generation through biological reproduction.

Genetically programmed algorithm. In the caste animal society, the response of the individual to identified social stimuli is also genetically determined. Metaphorically, the behaviors of all caste members are governed by an inherited "operating manual" consisting of "sequences of decision rules" (Holldobler and Wilson 2009: 54):[11]

> The program unfolds in linear manner. As each successive binary decision point is reached, the individual colony member proceeds down one pathway or another until it comes either to the next decision point or to the end of the sequence … A complete sequence of decision points that produce a caste, product, or full behavioral response is called an algorithm.

This "operating manual" dictates the social responses of individual ants in a colony. Learning does take place over the short span of an ant's life, but, for the most part, the response algorithm for group collaboration in a caste society is genetically programmed, hence "hard-wired."

The possession of the self by the individual member is not needed in the caste animal society because all social activities are organized at the group level, and the inherited genetic algorithm is sufficient for directing conspecific collaboration among groups of individuals under various conditions.

6.3   Individualized society and individual recognition

Individualized animal societies are comprised of a smaller number of mutually acquainted individuals that collaborate with one another for survival and reproductive success. An individualized animal society bears the following characteristics: (1) individual recognition among social members, (2) relationships among members are influenced by histories of past interaction, and (3) collaboration among individuals is guided by habits imprinted through early life exposure and associative learning.[12] A paradigm example of the individualized society is the wolf pack.

Individual collaboration. In contrast to group collaboration in the caste animal society, social collaboration takes place at the level of individuals in the individualized animal society. The basic social unit of the individualized animal society consists of a mated pair and the pair's young offspring, with the larger individualized social units including multiple matrilines of adult female kin, their young offspring, and multiple adult males. A wolf pack is typically composed of a breeding pair, one to six yearlings, and up to six pups.[13] Wolves interact with one another within a pack as individuals, "traveling, hunting, feeding, and resting together in a loose association, with bonds of attachment among all animals" (Mech 2003 [1970]: 38).[14] Adult members and yearlings collaborate in food acquisition, territorial defense, and protection from predation, among other things.

The collaborative activity is often led by the alpha male of the pack, who takes the initiative and is followed by the rest of the pack members. In group hunting, wolves approach their prey using the four-step technique of "stalk, encounter, rush, and chase" that "is usually the same each time" (Mech 2003 [1970]: 199).[15] Although their attack technique is rather simple, hunting together as a pack enables wolves to capture and kill large animals that would be impossible to take down if hunting alone.

Individual recognition. Just as the caste society requires group identification, "animals with individualized societies require a system for individual recognition" (de Waal and Tyack 2003: 258).[16] Individual recognition is essential for the individualized society because it is needed for virtually every type of social activity in that society: from mate selection to pair bonding to the care of young. In the caste society, offspring care is the responsibility of the entire community and labor is divided among different task groups, but in the individualized society, reproductive functions are performed by individual parents who must recognize their own offspring in order to deliver care to them. Individual recognition is also crucial for the establishment and maintenance of the individual-level dominance hierarchy which is a prominent organizational feature of the individualized society. Without being able to recognize social members individually, conspecifics living in the individualized society would have to fight against each other all the time for food, mates, and other valuable items.

Individual recognition is accomplished differently in different individualized societies. Some animal species rely on smell and others use hearing to discriminate individual members. It is also common for vertebrates to use multiple sensory cues for individual identification. Wolves identify each other mostly by smell. Each wolf has its own unique scent, and the superior odor-detecting ability of the dog family enables wolves to identify each other "within three hundred yards downwind" (Mech 2003 [1970]: 15).[17] Wolves have a great sense of hearing as well and can detect each other's howling from miles away.

Emotions play a pivotal role in the formation of the wolf pack. There is a critical three-month window of time after the birth of the pups for pack members to establish emotional attachment to one another that lays the foundation for "the formation or continuation of the pack" (Mech 2003 [1970]: 133).[18] Collective denning during this three-month period allows individual members to forge a strong emotional bond that holds the wolf pack together for years.

Associatively learned habits. Unlike the genetically programmed "decision rules" that govern the social responses of the members of caste society, response algorithms in the individualized society are mostly imprinted on the young through early life exposures. Wolf pups stay with their adults in the den for three or more weeks after birth, followed by a period of socialization in which they learn the rules of social behavior from their parents and through interacting with their littermates. For example, individual members attain their ranks in the dominance hierarchy through repeated fighting in their early encounters, and once the pecking order has been established, the dominance hierarchy determines "order of access to food, mates, resting sites, and other objects promoting survivorship and reproductive fitness" with no more fighting among the individuals (Wilson 2000 [1975]: 11).[19] However, certain behavioral patterns might be "hard-wired." For instance, there appears to be an individual "ownership rule" that overrides the pecking order of the dominance hierarchy when it comes to food access. A subordinate wolf can prevent the higher-ranking conspecifics from taking food that it already possesses: "There seems to be an 'ownership zone' within about one foot of a wolf's mouth, and anything within that zone is beyond dispute" (Mech 2003 [1970]: 71).[20]

The self is not needed in the individualized animal society either. The rules for conspecific collaboration are learned in early life, requiring no more than group and individual recognition, and those rules are sufficient for the survival and reproductive success of the individuals. The stability of the environment in which individualized animal societies are embedded creates the "social inertia" (Wiley et al. 1999)[21] that enables individual members to collaborate with one another based on the shared behavioral habits linked to memories of past encounters.

6.4   Alliance society and self-recognition

The alliance society, also known as the fission-fusion society, is a subset of the individualized animal society characterized by a constant change of coalition among individual members. An *alliance* is a coalition of two or more individuals collaborating with one another to achieve a common goal. In an alliance society, individuals switch their allegiance and reconstruct coalitions from time to time based on their perception of the changes in the situations they encounter. Constant situational assessment and the corresponding coalitional adjustment require a new form of social identification and a new type of response algorithm that call for self-recognition, in addition to group and individual recognition. A paradigm example of the alliance society is the chimpanzee community.

Situational collaboration. Individuals in the alliance society collaborate with one another in a more flexible way. Situational coalitions are transient, do not always involve the same individuals, and the role each individual plays in a coalition may vary depending on situational requirements. This flexibility in alliance formation makes it possible for different individuals to collaborate for different tasks under different conditions. Chimpanzees live in an alliance society. The basic social unit of chimpanzees is "a loose consociation of about 30 to 80 individuals that occupy a persistent and reasonably well-defined home range over a period of years" (Wilson 2000 [1975]: 539).[22] Like wolves, chimpanzees are also male philopatric, with females leaving their natal group at puberty when they are about ten years old. But, unlike the wolf pack which has a stable social structure, the chimpanzee community is a loose association of related individuals within which temporary alliances form and break up with great fluidity.

Adult chimpanzee males often forage for food alone. However, they come together for territorial defense and meat hunting, and they also engage in political maneuvering to move up the dominance hierarchy. Temporary alliances with other males are formed through meat sharing and allogrooming, and the coalition of two lower-ranking individuals may overthrow the alpha male. In cooperative hunting for their favorite prey such as the colobus, individual chimpanzees cooperate by playing highly differentiated hunting roles which include drivers, blockers, chasers, and ambushers. The successful performance of these roles requires each hunter to "anticipate not only the actions of the prey, but also the effect the action of other chimpanzees will have on the future movements of the colobus" (Boesch 2002: 34).[23] It is in this type of situational collaboration, which is more flexible and complicated than the observance of habitual rules in the individualized society, that the possession of the self by the individual becomes a necessity.

Self-recognition. The self is the entity one perceives to be one's own existence and that self-perception is influenced by others' attitudes toward oneself. To recognize oneself in social interaction, the individual must have the capacity to accomplish the following: (1) to recognize others, not just the physical attributes of others but also others' mental states such as intentions and attitudes; (2) to recognize others' intentions and attitudes in relation to oneself, e.g., what others want one to do or not to do; and (3) to indicate to others one's own intentions and attitudes in relation to them; that is, what one would like them to do or not to do. In the literature, this high-level mental capacity has also been referred to as "triadic awareness":

> Just as individual recognition is a prerequisite of a stable hierarchy, so is *triadic awareness* a prerequisite of a hierarchy based on coalitions ... What is special about this kind of knowledge is that an individual is not only aware of his

or her own relationships with everyone in the group, but also monitors and evaluates relationships that exist in the social environment so as to gain an understanding of how the self relates to *combinations* of other individuals. (de Waal 2007 [1982]: 175).[24]

Self-recognition is therefore the highest level of social identification, with group recognition at the lowest level and individual recognition at the middle level. Individuals of a species capable of a higher level of social identification are able to achieve social identification at the lower levels, but not the other way around.

Self-recognition requires a cognitive ability that animals in caste and individualized societies do not possess. All animals have the ability to recognize their somatic experience so that they can distinguish their own bodily experience from external environmental stimuli. At the next higher level, all social animals have the ability to recognize their relationship with conspecific others so that they can function properly in society. According to the capability of social animals to conceptually represent their intentional relations with others, Barresi and Moore (1996)[25] divide self-understanding into four levels, ranging from no conceptual representation to some representation to full representation. They put human self-awareness at level 4 and that of dolphins and great apes, including chimpanzees, at level 3. Social animals with level 3 self-awareness are capable of understanding intentional relations based on the current experiences they have with their conspecifics. In the absence of language, individual members gauge others' intentions and express their own relying exclusively on nonverbal cues, and they achieve self-recognition by seeing themselves "from the perspective of the other" (Barresi and Moore 1996: 114).[26]

Situationally established mutual expectations. Perceiving oneself from the standpoint of the other is necessary for conspecific cooperation in the alliance society due to the emergent nature of situational joint action. Genetically programmed rules and associatively learned habits are too rigid and inflexible to guide transient collaborations among individuals in an evolving and unpredictable environment. To form an alliance with another low-ranking individual against the alpha male, for example, the rebellion members must coordinate their high-risk activities carefully in accordance with the evolving situation, and any wrong move they make "can result in a significant increase or decrease in reproductive success. The latter might result from injury, a loss of rank, or expulsion from the social group" (Connor and Mann 2006: 337).[27] To engage in such situational collaborations, individuals need to convey on the spot what roles they expect each other to play and what rules of the game they must follow, but all this would be impossible to achieve without the cognitive capacity for self-recognition. As Boesch (2002: 29)[28] points out in describing chimpanzees' cooperative hunting:

> Collaboration requires the further elaboration of individuals understanding one another since in this case they performed different roles that are only possible if each considers the others' actions. Thus, in cooperation it is necessary to consider the perspectives of others.

The ability to communicate mutual expectations and negotiate contingent rules for joint action makes it possible for conspecific individuals to collaborate in transient and uncertain situations. And this is also the reason why the submodules for social identification at the group and individual levels become insufficient for conspecific collaboration in the alliance society.

6.5 Conclusion

All societies need a program of social identification, but not all societies need their members to have selves. The program of social identification allows the members of society to recognize the social stimuli they encounter so that they can act properly based on the response algorithm they have. The self is associated with a particular form of social identification necessary for a particular type of society. Social identification in the form of group recognition in the caste society and individual recognition in the individualized society is sufficient for animals to meet their cooperative needs in their respective environments. Self-recognition becomes a necessity for conspecific collaboration only in the fission-fusion society where individuals must specify role expectations for each other in the formation of contingent coalitions in evolving situations. The ability to take the attitudes of others toward oneself and regulate one's activity according to the negotiated mutual expectations makes situational collaboration among conspecific individuals possible in an alliance animal society.

Humans also live in the alliance society and engage in situational collaboration, but there is a critical difference in conspecific collaboration between humans and animals. While animals rely solely on nonverbal cues in communication, humans are capable of using syntactic language and this unique linguistic capacity fundamentally changes the dynamics of interaction among social members. In situational cooperative activity, language use makes the specification of role expectations more explicit and precise, which in turn facilitates more effective alignment and co-regulation of activities for collaboration. More importantly, use of language in combination with self-recognition give rise to the normative self that makes institution-based normative cooperative activity possible. Institutions are systems of rule specifications for cooperative activity created by social members based on the attitudes of the generalized other with which the normative self is associated. Individuals with normative selves are able to cooperate with one another according to institutional rules that overcome the uncertainty of situational contingencies.

According to the evolutionary biologist Edward Wilson, there appears to be a negative relationship between cooperativeness and individuality in animal societies: the higher the level of cooperation among members of society, the lower the level of individuality the members have. However, the possession of the language-based normative self catapults human cooperation to the highest pinnacle of social evolution that "approach[es] the insect societies in cooperativeness" and surpasses the chimpanzee communities in individuality (Wilson 2000 [1975]: 380).[29]

Notes

1. Part of the material discussed in this chapter comes from an article previously published by the author: Shanyang Zhao (2018) 'What is reflective self-awareness for? Role expectation for situational collaboration in alliance animal society,' *Philosophical Psychology*, 31(2), 187–209.
2. To be more precise, it is the ancestral environment to which a species was adapted that explains the current characteristics of the species. The alteration of the selection pressures associated with the ancestral environment will eventually lead to changes in the characteristics of the concerning species.
3. Shanyang Zhao (2018).
4. Edward O. Wilson (2000 [1975]) *Sociobiology: The New Synthesis*. Cambridge, MA: Harvard University Press.
5. For detailed descriptions of these three types of animal societies, see Shanyang Zhao (2018).
6. Edward O. Wilson (2000 [1975]).
7. Thomas D. Seeley (1995) *The Wisdom of the Hive: The Social Physiology of Honeybee Colonies*. Cambridge, MA: Harvard University Press.

8. Ibid.
9. Bert Holldobler and Edward O. Wilson (2009) *The Superorganism: The Beauty, Elegance, and Strangeness of Insect Societies*. New York: W. W. Norton.
10. Queens in the polygynous colonies are able to recognize each other individually. See Holldobler and Wilson (2009).
11. Holldobler and Wilson (2009).
12. Frans B. de Waal and Peter L. Tyack (eds.) (2003) *Animal Social Complex: Intelligence, Culture, and Individualized Societies*. Cambridge, MA: Harvard University Press.
13. Claudio Sillero-Zubiri, Dada Gottelli, and David W. Macdonald (1996) 'Male philopatry, extra-pack copulations and inbreeding avoidance in Ethiopian wolves (*Canis simensis*),' *Behavioral Ecology and Sociobiology*, 38, 331–340.
14. L. David Mech (2003 [1970]) *The Wolf: The Ecology and Behavior of an Endangered Species*. Minneapolis: University of Minnesota Press.
15. Ibid.
16. Frans B. de Waal and Peter L. Tyack (eds.) (2003).
17. L. David Mech (2003 [1970]).
18. Ibid.
19. Edward O. Wilson (2000 [1975]).
20. L. David Mech (2003 [1970]).
21. Haven Wiley, Laura Steadman, Laura Chadwick, and Lori Wollerman (1999) 'Social inertia in white-throated sparrows results from recognition of opponents,' *Animal Behavior*, 57, 453–463.
22. Edward O. Wilson (2000 [1975]).
23. Christophe Boesch (2002) 'Cooperative hunting roles among Tai chimpanzees,' *Human Nature*, 13, 27–46.
24. Frans B. de Waal (2007 [1982]) *Chimpanzee Politics: Power and Sex among Apes*. Baltimore, MD: Johns Hopkins University Press.
25. John Barresi and Chris Moore (1996) 'Intentional relations and social understanding,' *Behavioral and Brain Sciences*, 19, 107–154.
26. Ibid.
27. Richard Connor and Janet Mann (2006) 'Social cognition in the wild: Machiavellian dolphins?' in S. Hurley and M. Nudds (eds.), *Rational Animals?* Oxford: Oxford University Press, pp. 327–367.
28. Christophe Boesch (2002).
29. Edward O. Wilson (2000 [1975]).

Further reading

de Waal, Frans B. and Peter L. Tyack (eds.) (2003) *Animal Social Complex: Intelligence, Culture, and Individualized Societies*. Cambridge, MA: Harvard University Press.
Terrace, Herbert S. and Janet Metcalfe (eds.) (2005) *The Missing Link in Cognition: Origins of Self-Reflective Consciousness*. Oxford: Oxford University Press.

Wilson, Edward O. (2000 [1975]) *Sociobiology: The New Synthesis*. Cambridge, MA: Harvard University Press.

Zhao, Shanyang (2018) 'What is reflective self-awareness for? Role expectation for situational collaboration in alliance animal society,' *Philosophical Psychology*, 31(2), 187–209.

7   Epilogue to *The Sociology of the Self*

This book has provided a succinct but advanced introduction to the sociology of the self. Chapters 3, 4, and 5 constitute the core of this book. In Chapter 3, which addresses the question of *what the self is*, an emic conception of the self was presented; in Chapter 4, which addresses the question of *how the self is formed*, the impact of two social structural factors – social schemas and social resources – on the formation of the self was analyzed; and in Chapter 5, which addresses the question of *why the self matters*, the importance of the self for situational human cooperative activity and the institutional regulation of social life was explored. This concluding chapter is devoted to a highlight of the key arguments made in the book with some reflections on the implications of these arguments for personal well-being and sociological theorizing.

The self is a part of the self-phenomenon. The self of the individual is a component of a larger constellation of interrelated phenomena called the "self-phenomenon," which consists of (a) the empirical existence of the individual in society (i.e., one's corporeal, material, spiritual, and behavioral existence), (b) the self-concept of the individual (i.e., one's mental representation of one's own empirical existence); (c) the self-action of the individual (i.e., one's self-conscious efforts to manage one's own existence in society); and (d) the individual's self proper (i.e., the entity one perceives and acts toward as one's own existence). These four components are connected by three psychosocial processes – self-reflection, self-regulation, and self-verification (conceptual adjustment and self-enactment) – to form a self-directed feedback system that guides the activity of the individual in society. This conception of self recognizes the complexity of the self-phenomenon, linking the self proper to a set of related components and processes rather than pitting it against them. To have a self is to have all those parts including the relationships among them, and to understand the self is to understand the self-phenomenon as a whole. However, the word "self" can also be used in a narrow sense to refer to just the self proper.

The self proper is the individual's perceived own existence. As a subcomponent of the self-phenomenon, the self is not the same as one's empirical existence because the self is the perception of reality rather than the reality itself. What one really is constitutes a first-order object existing in itself, which can be perceived etically by others or emically by oneself. The self is not equal to one's self-concept either. Although perception is unavoidably influenced by preconception, one's perception of one's own existence can be at variance with one's preconceptions of oneself. Besides the influence of one's self-concept, the actual characteristics of one's empirical existence also have an impact on one's self-perception. What one perceives to be oneself is therefore the outcome of the interaction between what one really is (i.e., one's empirical existence) and what one believes one is (i.e., one's self-concept). The wisdom of self-understanding thus lies in the grain of salt one puts in one's self-concept and the sharp eye one keeps out for the changes in one's empirical existence. To know oneself is to embark on a voyage of self-exploration and self-discovery, on which one seeks to debunk one's own self-deception, correct one's self-myopia, and act as the Columbus to one's existence in society.

The self is an entity to be enacted. The self is not just an entity one perceives to be oneself, but also an entity one acts toward as one's own existence. In that sense, to *have* a self is to maintain the perception one has of oneself, and this perception-maintenance effort involves the process of self-verification in which one seeks to make sure one's self-concept corresponds to one's self-perception in everything one does. Perceived inconsistencies between the two are to be removed by either changing one's self-concept to align it with the perceived reality (i.e., conceptual adjustment) or to alter the perceived reality to make it match one's self-concept. In the latter case, the change in self-perception is accomplished by altering the empirical existence one perceives to be one's own through one's self-conscious action. This process is called self-enactment, which is the effort one makes to be what one thinks one is, can or ought to be. In essence, it can be argued that the self is not something one finds; rather, it is something one creates, maintains, and transforms. Without the possibility for enacting one's self, self-understanding and self-knowledge would be useless, for the very point of trying to know oneself is to better oneself.

The self is shaped by society. One's ability to enact one's self is conditioned by one's embedment in society. Society shapes the self of the individual in two important ways: (a) by influencing the formation of the individual's self-concept through the promulgation of social schemas, and (b) by affecting the individual's execution of self-action through the allocation of social resources. Depending on their situatedness in society, individuals are exposed to different social schemas and have access to different social resources, which result in the differential abilities individuals have for self-enactment. To fully understand the impact of society on the constitution of the self of the individual, it is necessary to go beyond the attitudes of significant others at the micro level to examine the influences of the generalized other at the macro level in the promulgation of social schemas and the distribution of social resources.

The self is biographically constituted. The self is both socially embedded and biologically embodied, so the biological embodiment of the self also has an impact on the constitution of self. The biological body hosts the brain that serves as the neurocognitive foundation for self-reflection and self-regulation; the biological body provides the inner needs, drives, and emotions that motivate the individual to interact with the environment; and the biological body has a finite lifespan that starts with the birth and ends with the death of the individual. The interaction between the individual's biological embodiment and social embedment of the self in the life course of the individual within society constitutes the *biographical experience* of the individual that shapes the formation of the individual's self. To fully understand the constitution of self, it is therefore also necessary to examine how the social embedment of the individual interacts with the biological embodiment of the individual in the context of the biographical experiences of the individual.

The self is indispensable to society. The reason individuals in human society and in the societies of certain select animal species come to possess selves is that collaborations among conspecifics in these societies require individuals to be self-reflective and self-regulative. Such collaborations make those species better adapted to their respective environments for survival and thrival. In human society, the possession of the self enables the individual to engage in situational cooperative activity at the micro level and normative cooperative activity at the macro level. The ability to take each other's perspectives and to regulate one's own behavior according to the expectations of others renders it possible for human individuals to collaborate in unpredictable, evolving situations as well as in institutionalized stable environments. Indeed, human society is constructed, maintained, and transformed by collaborative individuals with reflective self-awareness, and if there were no self there would be no human society. However, the selves of different individuals have different impacts on society, and such differences primarily reflect the variations in the individuals' situatedness in the structures of society.

This conceptualization of self introduced in the book has important implications for sociological theorizing. One of the central theoretical problems sociologists have been tackling for a long time is the linkage between individual action and social structure, which is also known as the "micro–macro linkage" or "agency-structure" problem. Human individuals are agentic agents who self-consciously direct their own action, but social structure, such as institutional rules and norms, has the constraining power to regulate individual behavior. How can the agency and freedom of the individual be theoretically reconciled with the regulative power of social structure? The concept of the emic self can shed some new light on this age-old issue.

All societies must solve the problem of how to hold separate individuals together for collaborative activity, or there would be no society. The possession of the self by the individual is one of the solutions to such a problem. In a caste animal society, this problem is resolved by hard-wiring genetically programmed algorithms into the individuals through biological reproduction; and in an individualized animal society, the problem is resolved by imprinting associatively learned habits on the individuals through early life exposure. In these two instances, individuals do not have much agency and freedom in determining the structures of their societies. In the case of an alliance animal society, situational self-awareness provides individuals with the agency to forge transient coalitions with conspecifics based on situational calculation and mutual expectations; however, the freedom the individual attains is at the expense of the stability and the regulative power of society. The chimpanzee community, for example, essentially becomes a loose association of semi-solitary individuals.

In human society, the normative selves enable the construction of institutional rules and regulations that hold competing individuals together for cooperative activity beyond the realm of physical copresence. Given that institutions are created, maintained, and transformed by human individuals themselves, institutional regulation of individual behavior is nothing but human self-regulation, a manifestation of human agency. Needless to say, not all human individuals possess the same amount of agency to impact their society because individual agency is conditioned by the individual's location in social structure: those in decision-making positions have more power to regulate the lives of others. The issue of human agency and social structure thus comes down in part to the issue of power; namely, who regulates whom. It also has to do with the impact of human tradition and history, as what predecessors did in the past comes to condition what their successors can do in the present, in which case the issue of agency versus structure becomes a matter of how much the dead affect the living. In all those cases, it can be seen that the institutional regulation of social life in human society is an expression of the agency of self-conscious human individuals, and the tension between social structure and individual agency is in fact the tensions among humans themselves. The so-called agency and structure problem should therefore be reframed as a problem of how self-conscious humans come to regulate their social lives under given historical conditions.

A related issue is the role individuals play in human history. If humans had no selves, human societies would have no history because the development of human society would be entirely determined by factors that humans have no control over. However, the possession of selves enables human individuals to play an active role in influencing the trajectory of their societal development. This agency is exercised by every human individual in society, but the social impact of individual agency is greater for those in leadership positions, and the self-conscious decisions made by individuals in key positions at a critical juncture or tipping point of social transformation can influence the direction of history. This factor contributes to the openness and uncertainty inherent in the development of human history, which is something that sociologists need to take seriously in theorizing societal change.

In conclusion, to understand human society it is necessary to understand human selves, and to understand human selves it is necessary to understand human society. In other words, it is as important to examine the impact of self on society as to examine the impact of society on self. Recognition of the reciprocal relationship between self and society is essential to the development of a sound sociological theory. This book has introduced a new conceptual framework for the sociological study of the self. As the knowledge of self and society increases, the framework introduced in this book will need to be revised and further improved on, a task that will fall in part on the shoulders of the readers of this book.

Index

joint attention 81
language 83–4
normative cooperative activity 84
operating manuals or algorithms
83
shared intentionality 81
situational cooperative activity 84
steps 81
we-intention 82
Human Nature and the Social Order
(Cooley) 2

impression management 72
indexicality 88
individualized society and recognition
associatively learned habits
109–10
collaboration and recognition
108–9
emotions 109
ownership zone 110
social inertia 110
institutional entrepreneurs 72–3
inter-organism behavior regularity
13–14
interpretive adjustment 43
iteration of self-verification 46–7

James, William 1–2, 45
joint action 81
joint attention 81

language 83–4
lateral comparison 63
see also social comparison
left inferior frontal gyrus (LIFG) 54
level 3 self-awareness in animals 112
linguistic communication 29

Markus, Hazel 33
McIntosh, Donald 38
Mead, George H. 2, 68, 85
mechanisms, relationships among 58,
67–9
absolute and relative concordance
69

concordance of social schemas
68–9
cross-mechanism inconsistency
69
mechanism of social comparison
68
sequential ordering 58, 67
me-ness or mineness concept 20
midlife crisis in adults 44
Mind, Self, and Society (Mead) 2
Mischel, Walter 41
Modernity and Self-Identity (Giddens)
4
Moore, Chris 112
moral reasoning 35
Morf, Carolyn C. 41
multidisciplinary endeavors 15

Neisser, Ulric 24
neolithic revolution 99
neurocognitive capacities 52–4
conceptual self-awareness 53–4
perceptual self-awareness 53
prerequisites 7
self-reflection 53
self-regulation 54
normative cooperative activity and
self 90–4
aligning action 92
altercasting 92–3
institution 90
institutional construction 91–2
institutional functioning 92–3
institutional transformation 93–4
normative cooperative activity 90
normative self 90
self-monitor and self-adjust 92
syntactic language 90
normative self 7, 9, 80, 90–2, 114
normative self-awareness 80, 99
Nurius, Paula 33

Olson, Eric 24
operating manuals
in animals 107
or algorithms 83
others, types 3
ownership zone in animals 110

urban sociology 15
see also sociology

veracity of self-knowledge 45
verbal communication 55, 83, 89

Weber, Max 12
we-intention 82
we-mode in cooperative activity 94–8
    collaboration and competition 96
    definition 94
    'I' mode 95
    "me" 96–7

normative us 96
over-socialized 97
selves of individuals 97
situational us 96
social schemas and social
    resources 55–6, 97
societal functions of self 97
    see also social schemas and
        self-concept
Wilson, Edward 114
within-mechanism inconsistency 68

Zahavi, Dan 19–20

Titles in the **Elgar Advanced Introductions** series include:

International Political Economy
Benjamin J. Cohen

The Austrian School of Economics
Randall G. Holcombe

Cultural Economics
Ruth Towse

Law and Development
Michael J. Trebilcock and Mariana Mota Prado

International Humanitarian Law
Robert Kolb

International Trade Law
Michael J. Trebilcock

Post Keynesian Economics
J.E. King

International Intellectual Property
Susy Frankel and Daniel J. Gervais

Public Management and Administration
Christopher Pollitt

Organised Crime
Leslie Holmes

Nationalism
Liah Greenfeld

Social Policy
Daniel Béland and Rianne Mahon

Globalisation
Jonathan Michie

Entrepreneurial Finance
Hans Landström

International Conflict and Security Law
Nigel D. White

Comparative Constitutional Law
Mark Tushnet

International Human Rights Law
Dinah L. Shelton

Entrepreneurship
Robert D. Hisrich

International Tax Law
Reuven S. Avi-Yonah

Public Policy
B. Guy Peters

The Law of International Organizations
Jan Klabbers

International Environmental Law
Ellen Hey

International Sales Law
Clayton P. Gillette

Corporate Venturing
Robert D. Hisrich

Public Choice
Randall G. Holcombe

Private Law
Jan M. Smits

Consumer Behavior Analysis
Gordon Foxall

Behavioral Economics
John F. Tomer

Business and Human Rights
Peter T. Muchlinski

Spatial Statistics
Daniel A. Griffith and Bin Li

The Sociology of the Self
Shanyang Zhao